齊物
逍遙
2019

黃效文——著

ENLIGHTENED
SOJOURN

Authored and Photographed by Wong How Man

Wong How Man

Time Magazine honored Wong How Man among their 25 Asian Heroes in 2002, calling Wong "China's most accomplished living explorer". CNN has featured his work over a dozen times, including a half-hour profile by anchor Richard Quest. Discovery Channel has made several documentaries about his work. The Wall Street Journal has also featured him on its front page.

Wong began exploring China in 1974. He is Founder/President of the China Exploration & Research Society, a non-profit organization specializing in exploration, research, conservation and education in remote China and neighboring countries. Wong has led six major expeditions for the National Geographic. He successfully defined the sources of the Yangtze, Mekong, Yellow River, Salween, Irrawaddy and the Brahmaputra rivers.

His organization conducts nature and culture conservation projects covering China and neighboring countries, including India, Nepal, Bhutan, Laos, Myanmar, the Philippines, and also Taiwan. Wong has authored over thirty books and has received many accolades, among them an honorary doctorate from his alma mater, the University of Wisconsin at River Falls, and the Lifetime Achievement Award from Monk Hsing Yun of Taiwan. He has been keynote speaker at many international functions.

黃
效
文

《時代雜誌》曾選黃效文為亞洲二十五位英雄之一,稱他為「中國最有成就的在世探險家」。CNN 報導過黃效文的各項工作超過十二次之多,其中還包括主播 Richard Quest 的三十分鐘專訪。探索頻道也為他做的工作製作了好幾個紀錄片。《華爾街日報》也曾用頭版報導過他。

黃效文自一九七四年開始在中國探險。他是中國探險學會的創辦人和會長,這是個非營利組織,致力於在中國偏遠地區及鄰近國家的探險,研究,保育和教育工作。他曾經在美國《國家地理雜誌》帶領過六個重要的探險。他成功地定位的源頭包括長江,湄公河,黃河,薩爾溫江,伊洛瓦底江及雅魯藏布江。

他的學會主導的文化和自然保育項目橫跨中國和鄰近的國家,包括印度、尼泊爾、不丹、寮國、緬甸、菲律賓還有台灣。

黃效文著作的書超過三十本並獲得過許多榮譽,他的母校威斯康辛大學頒發給他名譽博士學位,星雲大師也贈與他「華人世界終身成就獎」。他也是許多國際會議裡的專題演講人。

Preface

So the journey continues. I always believe there are ups and downs in life. But even when down, I want to be there with style. When on a low ebb, I often reminded myself that I must not only pull through, but with style, like an artist.

I remember being exhausted from a 74-kilometer bike ride. But, while the body was tired out, I nonetheless dwelled on inhaling the air when cycling through Maotai of Guizhou, full of aroma of the infamous white liquor. Breathing its fragrance was both intoxicating and exhilarating.

And if I were hell bound, I want to seek my own way in getting there, not being led there by others, or being pulled down to purgatory. At times, I become somewhat cynical and sarcastic. When friends told me they are depressed, I would say, "enjoy your depression". The best romance is written when two persons are apart, not together. Much of the greatest art, music, or literature, are created when under the spell of a depression, not high as if dancing in the clouds.

So, it was recently when my computer crashed while in the field, infested with ants in Myanmar, that I should feel quite low. However, I modified my attitude from efficiency to efficacy - as an art, scripting by hand. After all, I was trained since childhood in penmanship. Later I graduated to the use of a manual typewriter at Journalism School, punching keys of the likes of an Underwood or a Smith Corona. While working in the field as an explorer, I used a German portable Olympia.

By 1981, I saw a professor friend James Lee who taught Chinese history at Caltech using a portable computer, the Osborne. It had a three-inch black and white tiny monitor run on floppy disks. I decided to go upmarket and began lugging the 26-pounds behemoth around. I used Wordstar for the next two decades, seeing me into the portable PC and Laptop age, until the program became totally obsolete.

It helps somewhat that one of my best friend's company accounted for the design and manufacturing of over one-third of the world's notebook computers, allowing me to reduce weight while adding functions and memory into the modern age. That perhaps resonance my style, always on the edge, at times toward the extreme, covering both sides of the spectrum.

Finally, I am returning to basic in handwriting this Preface. More or less the 30th one I have written over the years. Nonetheless, it would not diminish the content of this new and continuing journey, with some of my personal style. The articles in this latest book cover a diverse field and geography of my recent travels, some in exploration, others a bit less adventurous. Enjoy.

序

旅程依舊持續進行。我一直相信人生中有高潮也有低潮。即使在不如意的時候，我也會用自己的方式去面對。低潮時，我總是提醒我自己，不僅要熬過這個難關，還要像個藝術家一樣用屬於自己的風格去面對。

我記得騎了七十四公里自行車時的精疲力盡。儘管身體如此疲倦，經過貴州茅台時，我還是很享受空氣裡茅台的酒香。醉人也同時令人振奮的香氣。

即使要去地獄，我也要用我自己的方式到那裏，我不要被別人牽著鼻子走，或是被拖著去煉獄。有時候我會有點反諷或是挖苦。當朋友跟我說他們很憂鬱時，我會跟他們說「享受你的憂鬱」。最浪漫的愛情故事裡，倆個人都是分離的，而不是在一起的。最出色的藝術、音樂或是文學很多都是在憂鬱的狀態時被創造出來的，而不是飄飄然地，開心地在雲端跳舞那樣。

最近我的電腦在緬甸被螞蟻入侵掛點，我當然覺得很憂鬱。但是我選擇修正我的態度，從有效率到有效能；我開始用手寫，手寫可是門藝術。畢竟我從小就練習書寫。我在讀新聞系時使用手動打字機，用安德伍德打字機或是史密斯牌打字機打字。做為一個探險家在野外時，我用德國製攜帶式的奧林匹亞打字機。

一九八一年我見到在加州理工學院教中國歷史的 *James Lee*（李中清教授）使用一台攜帶型的 *Osborne* 電腦，三吋黑白螢幕加上軟性磁碟的電腦。我於是決定升級到 *Wordstar* 寫作軟件，那可是個二十六磅的龐然大物。二十年間我用這軟件進而至攜帶式個人電腦，之後是筆電到處征討，直到這軟件被淘汰為止。

擁有市占率超過全球三分之一的筆電製造商，正是我的一位摯友，他讓我的筆電更現代化，擁有更強大的功能和記憶容量，但是重量卻越來越輕。這正是我的風格，總是跑在最邊緣，有時甚至顯得很極端的兩極。

最後，我回到用筆親手書寫這篇序言。這篇差不多是這些年來我所寫的第三十篇自序了。我持續用我自己的風格繼續我的旅程。這本書裡的文章涵蓋了各種領域和近期旅行的疆界地域，有些更是探險時的新發現，無論是哪個部份，都希望你享受其中。

目次

令人懷舊的獵鷹 *1984*

HUNTING-EAGLE REMINISCENCE

Hong Kong – October 26, 2018

HUNTING-EAGLE REMINISCENCE 1984

Over my decades of exploration in China, I twice had the opportunity to observe hunting-eagles up close. First was in 1984 when I was with the National Geographic and traveled to Akqi along Xinjiang's border with the then Soviet Union, and stayed among Kirgiz people. That experience was the most unique as I was allowed to ride out with a group of men with their eagles for a hunt. The second time, less significant, was in 1996 during a visit to northern Xinjiang with the Kazak.

Using golden eagles and falcons to hunt was an age-old tradition among Central Asian people, including the Kirgiz, Kazak, extending to Mongolia and even among the Manchus in the past. Hunting was most active in late autumn into winter. Though out of season in late September during my visit, I was feasted not only to freshly slaughtered sheep, but also had an insider look at the hunting-eagle's anatomy and dynamics.

The border "commune" I visited was Sumutaxi, adjacent to the national frontiers of two giant communist countries. Following a festive event organized for this "rare" visitor from overseas, seven Kirgiz men rode up on horseback to the festive ground with giant golden eagles on their arms. One other man, rather than sporting an eagle, had a beautiful falcon instead. These smaller birds of prey were for small game like rabbit rather than after fox, blue sheep and even wolf.

Balancing eagle on horse / 帶著獵鷹在馬背上維持平衡

After a round of photography of these majestic looking riders with their eagles, I was given a chance to ride out with them, carrying in my heavily gloved right arm one of these eagles with a leather hood over its head. With a T-shaped rest for my arm over the front of the saddle, I had to maneuver the bridle with my left arm, not an easy feat for someone not grown up on a saddle. When I took off the thick arm-glove, I could see markings on my forearm, as when we rode I occasionally lost balance and my eagle would tighten its grip on my arm, thus leaving bruising marks. Fortunately, the outing was short and soon we returned to the village to hear the stories unveil from the mouths of these proud owners of hunting-eagles.

I found out that the eagle riding with me, an eight-year-old bird, was one of the champion hunters. It successfully hunted 17 foxes and 15 Blue Sheep the previous winter, netting its owner over 500 Rmb, given a fox skin was traded for about 20 to 30 Rmb at the time, whereas a finely trained and mature eagle could be traded for 300

Eagles at Kirgiz festival / 柯爾克孜族節慶裡的獵鷹　　　　　　　HM go hunting / HM 去打獵

Rmb. Only fox skin were sold whereas wild sheep were retained for self-consumption and use. Throughout Akqi county, there may be over 150 families raising hunting-eagles, with a few having one of four kinds of minor falcons. Eagles between the age of four to eight years old are the best hunters.

I interviewed 37-year-old Kumashi, a Kirgiz living three kilometers east of town. His eagle named "Bosom", meaning fully grown at two years, had been with him for four years. At times eagles are named according to the hill or ravine they were caught. Others may be named due to their characteristics. Kumashi caught his bird some years back while herding sheep. At the time, it was about one year old and stood 1.5 feet tall. Birds were usually born in the summer and he caught it the following year when it was starting to learn to hunt in the wild.

They were usually caught within two months after the young adult birds learned to fly and hunt. At that time, leaving their nest and mother for the first time, such birds were not experienced. They

A hooded eagle and Kirgiz / 戴上眼罩的老鷹和柯爾克孜族

Hunting-falcon / 鷹隼

would usually eat too much after a successful hunt, became too heavy to take flight and could be caught easily by chasing them on horseback. The bird would fly and stop, until it was exhausted and could take flight no more and be covered by a huge winter coat to take home.

Another method was to wait until the parent birds left to fetch food and catch the baby birds from the nest. Two to three persons could lower the catcher with ropes down a cliff where the white dropping from the birds were obvious, giving evidence of an active nest. Such young chicks could then be raised at home for training when they reach one year old. Such home-raised birds are however generally noisier, as being young chicks in nests, they always cry for food to be fed, and never learned to stay quiet. As they became a family member of the household, they seem more spoiled, like a child, being hand-fed from chick to juvenile. It was said that a nest would have three, five or seven eggs, usually in odd number. An even number of eggs were said to be unlucky, often producing chicks that died young.

A third method is used to catch an adult bird. A pole around four feet high with a foot trap or snare would be set up on the ground. A trained eagle would be tied to the ground or another pole nearby, and a piece of raw meat or a small live animal like dove or chicken as bait would be put between the pole and the tied eagle. A wild eagle hovering above would catch the scene with its sharp eyes. Because another eagle on the ground can be a possible rival, the wild one would assess the situation carefully before homing in on its target. It would generally descend to rest and perch on the higher pole first. Once the eagle was tangled by the snare, the eagle catcher hidden nearby under camouflage of the surrounding bush would rush out to secure the captured bird.

It was said that the first and third methods of catching produce the best result, netting an adult wild bird. Such birds would always be afraid and a bit apprehensive of people, unlike those taken from the nest as young chicks and raised by hand. Birds taken from the same nest should avoid being on the same hunt after training. They are said to gang up and fight other eagles at times. However, the adult birds caught should be trained within three months of being caught. Training, or breaking, of an eagle requires patient and persistence. A long but light chain must be used to secure one foot of the eagle. Heavier metal beads would be used as anchor at the far end, allowing the bird to move and feed, but cannot fly away. A leather eye hood must be used to cover the bird's head, day and night, though it is left off during the summer and employed only before and during the hunting season, from October to March for a total of six months.

A hunting-eagle can live to be twenty years old. Some family would have up to three hunting-eagles. If there were babies within the household, some caution must be taken as at times eagles may attack tiny babies. Both male and female can be great hunters. Those within a family don't mate and don't fight, and would eat any raw meat, not considered costly given the economic return of the hunted prey. Kumashi's eagle hunted eight rabbits and eight fox last season. For this year, he intends to go after Blue Sheep. They rotate the hunted animals in order to allow the animals to be replenished.

An eagle is not released with its hood taken off until an animal is sighted or fresh footprints seen on the snow. Then a good horse can follow the flight of the eagle to go after the hunt. An eagle would catch a fox by the mouth, and a Blue Sheep by its ass. The largest game can be a wolf or even a big horn sheep. When a prey is caught, the eagle would never devour its hunt, but wait for the hunter to arrive. Usually a fox tail would be dragged behind the horse as a way to call home an eagle that would then return to its perch on the horse saddle. A small part of the meat of the prey must be given then to the bird for encouragement and incentive to secure the next hunt. One

Hood off eagle take flight / 拿掉眼罩的老鷹，展翅

must not feed an eagle until it is full. When full they are too heavy to take flight for a hunt and not eager for a kill.

Occasionally an eagle, after training and heading out for a hunt may take off and never return. First, those fed too well at home, may take off and never come back. Second, those with too heavy a chain that makes the eagle feel burdened and upset, may thus leaving and never return. Third is a bad and temperamental owner who treats the bird badly. This last type may even attack the owner before flying off.

Training of an eagle will probably be considered brutal harassment by animal rights advocates. First, you feed the eagle until it is fat and heavy. Such body weight, called "false strength" does not reflect real strength or stamina. It has to be turned into muscle before an eagle can become a real hunter. Next comes the "pulling of the fat" process. Starving it comes next, even "washing its stomach" as the locals called it, followed by giving the bird a warm bath to make it hot, sweaty and hungry. At times, the eagle would become so tired it rolls its eyes showing only the white part.

Then the eagle is put on top of a thick rope stretched between two poles. Of course, the eagle finds it difficult to balance, especially as the trainer keeps shaking the rope to disturb the eagle, which is soon flapping its wings wildly to retain balance. This is called "Sleepless exercise", prohibiting the bird to have any rest. Once the bird is fully exhausted and falls to the ground, the trainer would carry it and wash its head with water, and feed it with some tea and salt water to resuscitate it. Repeating such an act would thin the bird to only bones with barely any extra fat. Dispirited, the eagle could then be gradually trained with a hood on, feeding it bit by bit live rabbit, dove or other fowl. In time, the eagle would feel tied to its trainer and allowed to be tamed.

There are sixteen tail feathers to an eagle, allowing the bird to maneuver and steer in flight. These feathers would be tied up with thin strings accordingly, not too loose not too tight, such that the eagle could still fly but not for far. Live prey would also be tied in a yard and the hood taken off the hungry eagle so it would go after its prey. An eagle would first attack and take out the eyes of its prey before enjoying its meal. The trainer would grab away the prey repeatedly, then finally giving back some meat to feed the bird.

In time, the string on its tail would be removed one by one gradually, until the trainer is confident that the bird would not fly off. Usually it takes fifteen days or more to get through this training process. The release of the bird was first done indoor until the bird is used to returning to its master. When feeding, one should never fully feed an eagle and give only lean meat, not fat. That a fully-fed eagle would not hunt for a rabbit has become an idiom. Also until an animal is sighted, never take off the hood, so the eagle learns that once the hood is off, it expects to find prey. The metal chain is the last obstacle to a release.

For the Kirgiz, a good eagle is more valuable than a good horse. They felt such hunting activities were part of subsistence rather than a sport, though the communal outing would build bonds among men and pride for manhood. Hunting expeditions would involve at times over a dozen hunters with their respective eagles. That however was my reminiscence and notes from 35 years ago. Perhaps things have changed, especially with the One-Belt One-Road initiative. Back then, hunting-eagles were not part of tourism, not a lifestyle, but life itself, for the Kirgiz along China's western frontiers.

令人懷舊的獵鷹 1984

在中國探險的幾十年裡我有兩次機會近身觀察老鷹打獵。第一次是一九八四年，我在美國《國家地理雜誌》工作，沿著新疆和那時還是屬於蘇聯的邊境到阿合奇縣，在柯爾克孜族中生活。那次的經驗非常地特別，我跟一群男人帶著他們的鷹一起去打獵。第二次就是在一九九六年那一趟我跟哈薩克族人到新疆的北部。

中亞人，包括柯爾克孜人、哈薩克族到蒙古族甚至是歷史上的滿州族都有用金鷹和鷹隼打獵的傳統。深秋到剛入冬這段時間是打獵的季節，我在九月底到的時候其實已經過了季節，但當地人非常熱情地殺了一頭羊來招待我；我也剛好藉此機會深入了解獵鷹的身體結構和牠們飛翔的動力學。

我造訪了邊境的蘇木塔新 (Sumutaxi)「公社」，這裡位於兩個共產大國的前線。他們為了我這位遠從國外來的稀客舉行迎賓會之後，七位柯爾克孜男人騎著馬過來，他們的手臂上站著巨大的金鷹。而其中一位，帶來的不是老鷹而是一隻很漂亮的鷹隼。這種體型較小的鳥獵捕的對象是像兔子那樣的小動物，而不是岩羊或狼。

拍了一輪這些雄偉的騎士和獵鷹的照片後，我的右手臂戴上厚重的護具，上面站著一隻戴了皮革頭罩的獵鷹，我跟著他們一塊兒騎馬。T 型的扶手架在馬鞍前端，我必須要用左手來控制馬韁，這可不是一件容易的事，尤其是對我們這些不是在馬背上長大的人。當我把右手護具脫掉的時候，清楚看見小手臂全是瘀痕，因為只要在馬背上稍稍失去平衡時老鷹就會用力抓緊我的手臂，抓得我手臂上一塊塊的瘀青。幸好，這趟郊遊很短，很快地我們回到村裡，聽驕傲的獵鷹主人們述說他們的故事。

我帶的那隻老鷹已經八歲了，是隻頂尖的獵鷹。前一個冬季牠成功地捕獲過十七隻狐狸和十五隻岩羊，替主人賺了五百元人民幣，當時一件狐狸皮可以賣二十到三十人民幣，而一隻訓練有素的成鷹可以賣到三百人民幣。只有狐狸皮會拿出來賣，野羊的皮則是留下來自己用。整個阿合奇縣大約有一百五十戶人家飼養獵鷹，只有很少數的人有四種小鷹隼中的其中一種。四到八歲的老鷹是最好的獵鷹。

我訪問了一位三十七歲的柯爾克孜人 *Kumashi*，他住在離城鎮東邊三公里的地方。他的鷹叫「*Bosom*」，兩歲就完全長大，已經跟他四年了。那個時候，他們會根據捕捉到鷹的山丘或山溝來命名。也會以鷹的個性來命名。*Kumashi* 幾年前在放羊的時候抓到現在他的這隻鷹。那時候牠大約一歲半，一點五呎高。鷹通常在夏季出生，一歲大的時候剛好在學狩獵，*Kumashi* 就是在那時抓到了牠。

年輕的成鳥在剛開始學飛跟獵捕的兩個月之內很容易被捕捉。第一次離開母親和鳥巢，還不是很熟練，成功地獵到食物時會吃太多，變得身體太重不易飛行，在馬背上就可以輕易地抓到牠們。牠們會飛飛停停，直到體力耗盡，當再也飛不動了，就會被一件冬大衣罩住帶回家。

另外一種抓鳥的方式就是等鳥爸媽外出獵食時從鳥巢中抓幼鳥。從白色排泄物可以判斷這裡有活鳥巢，兩到三人會將抓鳥的人用繩索從懸崖垂降到有鳥巢處。幼鳥被帶回人類的家飼養，約一歲開始訓練。這時期的鳥通常都很吵，幼鳥總是哭叫著要食物，從學不會安靜。牠們成為家裡的一員，像個小孩一樣被寵，從幼鳥到成鳥都要親手餵食。據說一窩通常會有三顆、五顆、七顆蛋，都是單數，偶數不吉利，很多幼鳥都沒機會長大。

第三種方式是捕成鳥。一根四呎高的桿子裝上絆腳的圈套或陷阱，架在地上。然後會在地上或是鄰近的桿子上綁著一隻訓練過的老鷹，在牠前面放一塊生肉或是活的小動物，像鴿子或雞，當成誘餌。徘徊在上空眼力尖銳的老鷹將會看到這一幕，然後把在地上的這隻老鷹視為對手，牠會先小心地觀察再進一步瞄準目標。牠通常會先飛到桿子高處視察，但是一旦被牢籠纏上，躲在一旁的獵人就會馬上出來把老鷹抓住。

據說第一種和第三種方式捕捉野外的老鷹是最好的。這些老鷹會有些怕人，不像那些從幼鳥開始由人類親手拉拔長大的老鷹。同一窩的鳥不可以一起受訓，聽說牠們會集體跟其他老鷹打架。但是成鳥抓到後在三個月之內一定要開始訓練。訓練一隻老鷹需要耐心跟毅力。先用一條輕的長繩綁在鷹的一腳上，然後用有重量的金屬塊把繩的另一頭固定在地上，牠可以飛、可以獵食，但是飛不走。日夜都必須用一塊皮製眼罩蓋住眼睛，只有在夏季拿掉，在狩獵季節開始前和從十月到三月一共六個月都會用上。

獵鷹通常可以活到二十歲，有些人家會餌養到三隻。如果家裡有幼鳥的話，必須要小心成鷹可能會攻擊牠們。公的母的都可能是很厲害的獵鷹。養在家裡的不會交配也不會打鬥，牠們吃生肉，但是以牠們帶來的獵物來說，這經濟效益應還是划算的。*Kumashi* 的老鷹上一季獵到八隻兔子八隻狐狸。今年他想要獵捕岩羊。他們會輪流獵捕不同的動物，好讓其他的有機會繁殖。

當獵物或是腳印出現在雪地上時，鷹的眼罩才會被拿掉然後釋放。好馬會跟著天空中飛翔的老鷹走。老鷹會抓狐狸的嘴，岩羊的屁股。最大的獵物可能是一匹狼甚至是一隻大角羊。當捕到獵物時，老鷹不會吃牠們，牠會等獵人過來。獵人會將獵捕到的狐狸尾巴綁在馬的後面拖行，這是招回獵鷹到馬鞍架上的方式。一小部分的獵物一定要分給獵鷹當作獎賞，鼓勵牠們。但是千萬不能讓牠們吃飽，身體變重了不僅不易飛行，也不會專心打獵。

有時在訓練或打獵時，會發生一放出去就不回來的狀況。一種情況是，在家裡被餵的太好，一飛出去就不回來；第二種情況是，繩鍊太重了，讓老鷹感覺纍贅煩躁，這種也可能不會回來。第三種是脾氣不好的主人，對老鷹不好。對待這種主人，老鷹在飛走前可能還會先攻擊教訓主人一番。

訓練獵鷹的過程對動物保護人士來說可能是很殘酷的。首先要把鷹餵到夠胖夠重，這樣的體重稱為「虛假的力量」，並無法反應真正的力量或耐力。牠必須將這體重轉換成肌肉才能成為獵鷹。接下來是「脫脂肪」的過程－餓牠，當地人稱這叫「清胃」，然後再給鷹溫水浴，讓牠流汗，又熱又餓。這時候鷹會變得很累，眼睛出現翻白眼的症狀。

之後鷹會被放在一條綁在兩根竿子的繩子上。老鷹在上面不容易

Hunter of northern Xinjian / 新疆北部的獵人
Kazak with eagle / 哈薩克族和老鷹

站穩，馴鷹師還會不停地搖晃繩索，老鷹會用力扇動翅膀來維持平衡。這招叫做「無眠訓練」，不讓老鷹休息。一旦精力耗盡，就掉到地上，馴師會把鷹抱起來洗洗牠的頭，然後餵牠一些茶跟鹽水來喚醒牠。重複這樣的訓練會讓老鷹瘦到骨頭上幾乎沒有多餘的脂肪。鬱悶的鷹才會漸漸開始接受帶著眼罩受訓，然後一點一點餵牠活的兔子、鴿子或是野禽。一段時間後，老鷹就會被馴服。

鷹有十六個尾羽，在飛行時可以操控方向。這尾羽會被細繩綁住，不能綁的太緊或太鬆，讓鷹可以飛但是不能飛遠。活的獵物會被綁在院子裡，眼罩拿掉後，鷹一看見會去捕捉獵物。鷹首先會攻擊獵物，取下牠的眼睛準備飽餐一頓。但馴鷹師會反複拿走獵物，最後才給牠一點肉吃。

當馴鷹師覺得這隻鷹不會飛走的時候，才會把綁在尾羽上的繩子漸漸一步步解開。通常要花上十五天以上來完成這個訓練。先在室內練習放飛，讓牠們習慣回到主人身邊。只能餵食瘦肉，不能有肥肉，「飽腹老鷹不獵兔」早就是句成語。只有當獵物出現時，眼罩才會被拿開，所以老鷹知道這時牠要去獵物。金屬鍊是放飛的最後一關。

對於柯爾克孜人來說，一隻有用的獵鷹勝過一匹良馬。這樣的狩獵是他們生活的一部分，而不是休閒型的戶外活動，當時出去打獵要出動大約十二位獵人和他們的獵鷹，因此狩獵這樣的事會增進男人之間情感和男子氣概。這是我從三十五年前筆記本看到的過去。也許現在不同了，尤其加上一帶一路。獵鷹成為觀光的一部份，再也不是生活型態，但對歷史上的柯爾克孜人來說，它就是生活，對在中國西方邊境的其它民族來說亦如是。

Feeding an eagle / 餵食老鷹
Devouring fresh meat / 吞食鮮肉

葛倫堡和大吉嶺

KALIMPONG & DARJEELING

Thimphu, Bhutan – September, 2018

Thimphu, Bhutan – September, 2018

KALIMPONG & DARJEELING
In the Himalayan foothill

"I am sorry, your visa is only good for arriving by air, not by land. There are over thirty airports in India you can fly into," said the man in civilian clothes at the immigration office in the town of Jaigaon. Outside, there were a couple soldiers in uniform. They were seated and relaxing leisurely, with their rifles lying next to them. After all, this is a friendly and stable border.

I am deep inland at the land border of two Himalayan countries, just crossing into India from Phuentsholing Bhutan, where much traffic of goods and people of both countries cross every day. Big trucks, small pick-ups, motorbikes, push carts and foot traffic keep the crossing busy. The two towns are literally one, connecting to each other simply by a symbolic open gate crossing.

The Indian immigration office is deep inside town, not even in sight of the actual border. By the time I reached it I was several hundred meters inside Indian territory. The border "check point" simply waved us through, especially as I was traveling inside a Royal Palace car from Bhutan with a flag outside and a special red plate with golden lettering for a license.

13th Dalai throne room & shrine /
第十三世達賴使用過的佛堂和神龕

Her Majesty on right, How Man and Ashi Tashi /
皇太后陛下（右），HM 和 Ashi Tashi

Tenzin is my protocol officer, dispatched by the Foreign Ministry at the request of Her Majesty the Royal Grandmother of Bhutan who, at 88, has become my trusted friend within the last few years. The young man, fluent in English, has escorted many VIPs and dignitaries across the border from Bhutan into India, or vice versa. But none of those guests used a Chinese passport.

Tenzin suggests that we should simply head on to Bhutan House in Kalimpong, my destination for this trip. After all, we are already inside India, and I have a valid visa. Other particulars can be considered just minor and peripheral. I concurred as I felt no one had asked me to turn back, though the officer didn't feel he was entitled to put a stamp in my passport. If I must learn to live like a refugee or a fugitive for the next three days, so be it.

Many explorers preceding me had done worse, traveling without full permits. British agents and Indian pundits did it with impunity over a century ago, and their intrepid endeavors were read or written about by others with admiration. At that moment, one of my time-honored mottos came back into mind, "it is easier to ask for forgiveness than permission." Though I have heard that Indian prisons do not offer a pleasant experience.

The Elgin Silver Oaks hotel in Kalimpong offers a respite from the rice paddies, rubber plantations, and rain during the last stretch of windy road to our first destination at this hill station, once an important crossroad between Tibet and India. The hotel's architecture and immaculate service brought back memories of the old British colonial setting. Many old black and white pictures lined the hallway.

Kalimpong's role in history is precisely what brought me here to this enclave in the foothills of the Himalayas. The region used to be part of Bhutan, but was long ago ceded to British India. Traditionally the most influential family of Kalimpong was the Dorji family of western Bhutan, ancestor of the Royal Grandmother. But India inherited this land after its independence in 1947, when the British left.

The only traces of the Dorji and Bhutan's past is perhaps the venerable Bhutan House, a Victorian style bungalow with garden. British India gifted the estate to the Dorji family because of the role they played in connecting the British to Tibet around the turn of the 20th century. It has acted as both a residence and consulate for the kingdom of Bhutan. The Royal Grandmother of Bhutan was born in this house, and she is the fourth generation of the Dorji family to take up Bhutan House as her residence, previously belonging to her mother.

Elgin House / 埃爾金飯店   Waiter at the Elgin / 埃爾金飯店的服務生

Today it is used only once a year, during Losar or Tibetan New Year, when Her Majesty would grace Bhutan House with her presence and stay here, giving the traditional offerings to monks and monasteries around the region. For the rest of the year, the premises remain closed, guarded by Bhutan Royal Guards inside the premises, and Indian army/police guards on the outside.

But the story does not end there. In 1912, the 13th Dalai Lama fled Lhasa in Tibet during a very turbulent time right after the fall of the Qing Dynasty. He took up "shelter" or "residence" at Bhutan House for several months upon the invitation of Gongzim Kazi Ugyen Dorji, grandfather of the Royal Grandmother. This abode, specially built as temporary residence for the 13th Dalai in self-exile, resulted in a special friendship and relationship between the 13th Dalai and the Dorji family. The Dalai fondly called it "The place of unchanging supreme joy", which became the official honored and blessed name.

The shrine room where the Dalai stayed has been kept intact to this day, along with many relics, including a finely carved and engraved altar, a choesham (the only other like it remains in the Dalai Lama's room in the Potala in

Lhasa), with a throne seat. The large engraved altar is said to be a gift from the Qing Emperor, with the entire piece brought in by yaks and mules from Lhasa. A gold statue with the likeness of the 13th Dalai was placed upon the throne. As a traditional way to retrace steps of his predecessor, in later years, the 14th Dalai also visited and stayed at Bhutan House when he first went to India in 1956 to celebrate the Buddha's birthday, a few years before he left Tibet and went into exile.

Jigme, a nephew of Her Majesty living in Kalimpong accompanied me to visit Bhutan House. A full Bengal tiger pelt lying beside the entrance greets any visitors. Our first order of business was to make a pilgrimage to the shrine used by the 13th Dalai Lama, with his altar seat and many Buddhist statues still in place. It is a very solemn place. There are other deities inside several large cabinets encased in glass. A set of Kangyur, sacred sutras of Buddhism, are also kept within. A large pair of elephant tusks, yellow from age, stand guard on two sides.

With the attending army officer watching on the side, the caretaker brought out a long scroll of writing in Tibetan that the 13th Dalai had

Large scroll of the 13th Dalai / 第十三世達賴喇嘛書寫的長卷軸
Seals of the Dalai / 達賴的印章
Carved alter from China / 來自中國的聖壇

bestowed on the Dorji's. It has a very large red seal at the bottom. With care, he then took out a well wrapped box. In it were two seals of the 13th Dalai. Afterwards a Thangka was unrolled for my inspection. These are all considered very sacred relics that the Dalai had given to the family, and are rarely open to view.

There are old albums in the living room which I browsed through carefully. Many included pictures of the Dorji family and their growing up process. Others are of Her Majesty and her children of the royal family, many of whom were born and raised here. I took liberty and reproduced some of them for record. Numerous framed pictures are of the royal family of Sikkim where Her Majesty's mother came from. I was also taken on a tour of the entire house, including all the bedrooms and chambers on the second floor. I was told that at its prime, the premises held parties for guests several times a week. Many international guests and dignitaries had stayed here. Expeditions to Tibet, including several Everest expeditions, were flagged off from here. The Royal Grandmother had told me that adjacent buildings were used as the first English school for Bhutanese children. I felt extremely privileged, as few other visitors to Kalimpong would receive such care and private viewings.

Her Majesty had ordered the staff to prepare a special lunch, including

13th Dalai / 第十三世達賴喇嘛

Tiger at entrance / 入口處的老虎皮
Dining room for lunch / 用午餐的飯廳

selected wine, for my visit to Bhutan House. Jigme Tsarong, her nephew, is a member of the Tsarong family of Lhasa, very powerful before land reform, but Jigme had been educated and lived outside of Tibet for decades. He is also the son-in-law of Gyalo Thondup, the elder brother of the 14th Dalai Lama, a jetsetter and political dealmaker between Hong Kong, China, Taiwan, India and America.

Though both father and son in-law live in Kalimpong, they recently have had an estranged relationship, said to have arisen from certain differences regarding interpretation of Gyalo's history in his newly published memoir. Such intrigues are common in all families, but seem to especially fill the air with gossip when the players are either famous or secretive. Jigme treated me to high tea at his home up in the hills.

Along the way, we passed through a nice British era bungalow; Crookety House. This was once owned by Tashi, the elderly sister of Her Majesty, now at 95 years of age. Before that, it was the home of Nicholas and Helena Roerich, two very important yet little-known Russian explorers of Tibet. I can barely see the house, as the dense fog surrounded it, as if to help obliterate their very important contribution during a most trying winter journey through northern Tibet.

While in Kalimpong, I visited the famed Hatt Bazaar, a historic meeting place for merchants and traders from inside and outside of Tibet. In days past, Kalimpong was a booming trade center on the frontiers of Sikkim, Tibet and Bhutan. Horse trading was a major business for merchants, supplying the mule trains with draught animals to carry loads and cargo in and out of Tibet. Now such border trade has given way to a market place selling clothes, vegetables, eatables and knickknacks for daily use.

As Darjeeling is only a couple hours drive away, I decide to spend a day there. While others may come for the numerous tea plantations famed since the British days, my main focus is the narrow-gauge train that still runs with steam engines today. As we reached town, I was amazed to see how the train shared the narrow road with cars and pedestrians among the town's crowded buildings. This is certainly a novelty despite being well over a century old, first constructed in 1879.

Front of Bhutan House / 不丹館正面

Pastry of Glenary's / Glenary 的糕點

With tracks only two feet wide, it runs for 88 kilometers, rising from 100 meters in elevation to 2200 meters when it reaches Darjeeling. In 1999, it was declared a UNESCO World Heritage Site. At the terminal station, passengers were waiting for the next train to embark. I walked across the street to observe how the engineers were caring for one of those ancient steam engines. The huge billowing black smoke coming off its chimney reminded me of decades ago when I explored the northern forests of China where logging trains were all using steam engines. But then, their steam and smoke were largely white in contrast to these ink-like puffs from this train.

We stopped in town for high tea at the famous Glenary's Restaurant which makes wonderful pastry. It was recommended by Jigme. Later I went to the town square, but the famous Oxford bookstore was closed on Sunday and I was not able to get any of the books on the Himalayan region. I did manage to stop and browse through the large array of teashops dotting the town. No trip to Darjeeling can be considered complete without buying some tea as gifts to take home.

Now, the final trick would be re-entering Bhutan through the border, back to Her Majesty's Palace to report on my trip. But that again, I would leave to fate. With luck, I would not have to ask for forgiveness.

Traffic near Hatt Bazaar / 哈特市集附近的交通
Old tea shop / 老茶館

葛倫堡和大吉嶺

喜瑪拉雅山麓

「很抱歉，你的簽證只能從空港機場入境而不適用於陸路邊境。印度有三十幾個機場可以讓你飛進來的。」賈伊加奧恩鎮邊境身穿便服的移民官這樣對我說。而外面有兩位穿著制服的軍人坐在那裏，來福槍就放在他們身邊，看起來一派輕鬆的樣子。終究這裡是比較友善也比較穩定的邊境。

我剛從不丹的彭措林進入印度，開始深入喜瑪拉雅山這兩國的內陸邊境，這兩邊的人跟貨物每天都會穿梭在這個邊界。大卡車、小型貨車、摩托車、手推車、人潮讓這個邊境顯得十分熱鬧。其實這兩個城鎮根本就像一個城市，那個閘口只是象徵性的。

印度移民局在城裡，離真正的邊境口岸有點距離。而此刻我其實已經進入印度境內好幾百公尺了。邊境「檢查口」的人員揮手直接讓我們入境，我搭著不丹皇室的車一路前來，車外掛著一面旗杆還有一個特殊的紅色車牌，車牌上面的字還是金黃色的。

Tenzin 是我的禮賓官，他是皇太后陛下要求外交部派來的，八十八歲的陛下過去幾年和我成為彼此信任的朋友。這位年輕官員的英文很流利，接待過許多重要的外賓跟使節，護送他們從不丹跨過邊境進入印度或是從印度進入不丹。但是這些賓客沒有一個是用中國的護照的。

Hatt Bazzar 1930 / 哈特市集一九三零年　　　　　An exquisite Thangka / 精美的唐卡

Tenzin 建議我們直接去我此行的目的地：葛倫堡的不丹館。畢竟我們已經在印度了，而且我的簽證是有效的。其他的細節並不重要。我贊成直接去，因為沒有人要求我回頭，但是移民官卻不敢在我的護照上蓋章。如果接下來三天我要過得像個難民或是逃犯的話，那就順其自然吧。

在我之前的許多探險家做的比我過分多了，他們旅行時根本沒有完整的通行許可證。一世紀前英國特工和印度專家也做過同樣的事，後來他們令人敬佩的探險還被記錄下來，被世人廣傳。此刻我想到一直陪伴我的座右銘－「尋求寬恕比尋求許可容易」。不過我也聽說過印度監獄可能不會讓人留下愉快的經驗。

要先走過稻田、橡膠園、甚至歷經雨水與一段崎嶇的路才能抵達這家位於葛倫堡的埃爾金銀奧克斯飯店，這是我們在這山間驛站裡的第一個目的地，一個可以讓我們稍作喘息的地方；而這山間驛站曾經是往來西藏和印度之間重要的十字路口。這家飯店的建築和無微不至的服務讓人想起英國殖民地時期，飯店的走道還掛著許多以往的黑白照片。

Her Majesty with children / 皇太后陛下和她的小孩

葛倫堡在歷史上扮演的角色正是我來這裡的原因，這個位在喜馬拉雅山山麓的飛地（被包圍在另外一個國家境內）。這個地方曾經是屬於不丹的，但是許久前被割讓給了英屬印度。過去這裡最具影響力的是來自不丹西部的多吉家族，那是皇太后陛下的祖先。但是一九四七年印度脫離英國獨立後，就由印度繼承了這片土地。

關於多吉家族和不丹的歷史可能只剩下這棟珍貴的不丹館，是一棟維多利亞式的花園洋房。英屬印度贈送這棟房子給多吉家族，是為了感謝他們在二十世紀初期扮演西藏和英國中間人的角色。這棟是皇居也是不丹的大使館，不丹的皇太后陛下就是在這裡出生的，她是多吉家族的第四代，這裡曾是她的行宮，過去公館是屬於她母親的。

現在，一年一次的羅皇節或是藏曆新年時，皇太后陛下會來這裡，贈送供品給這區域附近的僧人和寺廟。而其他時間這裡是關閉的，內院由不丹皇家守衛看守，外面則由印度的軍警負責。

不過故事未完。就在一九一二年滿清政權剛剛結束後，第十三世達賴喇嘛在那個動盪的時代逃離拉薩。在皇太后陛下祖父的邀請下，達賴來到這裡「避難」或說是「居住」了好幾個月。這棟特別替第十三世達賴喇嘛流亡時短暫居住所蓋的房子，讓第十三世達賴和多吉家族建立起特殊的友情和關係。達賴親切地稱這裡為「永保喜悅之地」，這個被賜福的名字，後來亦被官方認證。

當時達賴待過的佛堂到今天仍保留著當年的樣貌，在眾多的文物中有一個雕刻精緻的聖壇，與寶座一起稱之為 choesham（唯一一件類似這個聖壇的文物現在在拉薩的布達拉宮，達賴喇嘛的房間裡）。據說這具規模的雕刻聖壇是清朝皇帝贈送的，整件雕刻一路從拉薩用氂牛和驢子運送到此。另有一座類似十三世達賴喇嘛的黃金雕像放在寶座上。第十四世達賴在流亡前也曾經造訪並住在不丹館這裡，一九五六年他跟隨十三世先人的腳步第一次去印度慶祝佛誕，幾年後就離開西藏開始流亡生涯。

皇太后陛下的侄子 Jigme 住在葛倫堡，是他陪同我去不丹館的。一整張孟加拉虎皮被放在門口迎賓，首先我們去第十三世達賴喇嘛用的佛堂朝聖，他用過的聖壇上許多佛像依然安在。這是一個很莊嚴的地方。好幾尊神佛放在大型玻璃櫃裡。另有一組甘珠爾和神聖的佛經也在裡面。有一對顏色已經泛黃的大象牙，像守衛般被放在兩旁。

Royal family pictures / 皇室家庭照

Framed pictures / 裱框的相片

在值班衛兵的看守之下，管理員小心翼翼地從包裝得非常好的盒子裡拿出一卷第十三世達賴喇嘛用藏文書寫給多吉家族的卷軸，紅色大印封蓋在盒子底部，還有兩枚達賴喇嘛的印章。然後他又攤開一張唐卡讓我欣賞。這些達賴贈送給多吉家族的文物是非常神聖珍貴的，鮮少拿出來供人參觀。

客廳裡有一些舊相簿，我在翻閱它們的時候非常小心。裡面有好多關於多吉家族成長過程的照片，還有皇太后陛下和她小孩的照片，好幾個孩子都是在這裡生長的。我擅自翻拍了幾張做紀錄。因為皇太后陛下的母親來自錫金，因此也有許多裱框的錫金皇室照片。他們帶我參觀整棟房子，包括所有在二樓的廳堂和臥室。據說，在全盛時期這裡每個星期都會舉辦好幾場接待貴賓的宴會。許多外國賓客和使節都住過這裡。不論是去西藏探險，或者前往珠穆朗瑪峰的旅途，都是從這裡出發的。皇太后陛下曾經告訴我，隔壁那幾棟曾經是不丹小孩的第一所英語學校。我感到非常榮幸，因為沒有幾個人到葛倫堡能受到如此的接待，並觀賞這些私人地方和藏品。

皇太后陛下請員工特別準備了午餐還有精選的葡萄酒在不丹館招待我。她的姪子 *Jigme Tsarong* 是拉薩 *Tsarong* 家族的一員，在土地改革前 *Tsarong* 曾經是非常強大的家族。*Jigme* 很早就離開西藏，在外地接受教育和生活了好幾十年。他也是第十四世達賴喇嘛哥哥嘉樂頓珠的女婿，嘉樂是一位穿梭於香港、中國、台灣、印度和美國的交易高手。

岳父和女婿都住在葛倫堡，只是最近關係有點疏離，因為雙方對最近出版的嘉樂回憶錄中關於流亡政府的故事有不同的詮釋。這種糾葛家家都有，但是當主角們是名人或是神秘的人時，總會讓人們津津樂道。*Jigme* 在他山上的家招待我喝下午茶。

路上我們經過一棟很漂亮的英國時期洋房叫「*Crookety House*」。這棟本來是 *Tashi* 擁有的，她是皇太后陛下的姊姊，現在九十五歲。更早之前這棟房子的屋主是 *Nicholas* 和 *Helena Roerich*，兩位非常重要卻鮮為人知的俄國探險家，是西藏的探險專家。濃霧圍繞讓我看不清楚這房子的樣貌，就彷彿歷史要抹去他們在嚴冬中穿越西藏北部的歷史。

我在葛倫堡去了著名的哈特市集，許久以來往來西藏的商人和貿易商都會來這裡交易。過去葛倫堡曾是錫金、西藏、印度和不丹的交易重地。馬匹的交易對商人來說是重要的生意，因為貨物必須靠著這些駝獸組成商隊進出西藏。如今邊境買賣的貨品已經變成衣服、蔬菜、食品還有日常用品。

既然開車到大吉嶺只要兩鐘頭，於是我決定去那裡一趟。其他人來這裡是為了從英國時期就很出名的茶葉，我則是為了直到現在還在用蒸氣引擎的窄軌火車。我非常訝異這火車竟然能穿梭在建築物林立的地方，跟行人、汽車共用一條狹窄的道路。一百多歲的火車，一八七九年蓋的，到現在仍然是很新奇的玩意。

它的軌道只有兩呎寬，八十八公里長，從海拔一百公尺到大吉嶺時已經來到海拔兩千兩百公尺。一九九九年聯合國教科文組織指定為世界遺產。乘客們在終點站等候下一班火車。我過街去看了

Posh Himalayan Princess carriage /
豪華的喜馬拉雅公主號車廂

工程師們是怎麼照顧這些骨董引擎的。一坨滾滾黑煙從煙囪冒出，讓我想到幾十年前我在中國北部的森林探險，那裏的伐木列車也是用蒸氣引擎。不過那時候的蒸氣和煙大多是白色的，跟這台冒出跟墨一樣的黑煙形成強烈的對比。

我們在城裡的一家很出名的 Glenary's 餐館喝下午茶，這裡的甜點做的很棒。這家店是 Jigme 介紹的。後來我去了城裡的廣場，本來想要買些關於喜瑪拉雅區域的書，可惜著名的牛津書店禮拜天沒開。書沒買成，但在城裡閒逛時倒是看到各式各樣的茶館。到大吉嶺沒買些茶當作禮物帶回家怎麼能算來過這裡呢。

來到最後一關，從邊境再入境不丹，回到皇太后陛下的皇宮跟她報告這趟旅程。不過還是讓命運決定，如果運氣好的話，我應該不用跟他人求饒。

Steam train in action / 行進中的蒸氣火車

Feeding coal into the burner / 添加煤炭到火爐裡

Sharing the road / 共享一條道路

奠
邊
府

DIEN BIEN PHU

Dien Bien Phu, Vietnam – October, 2018

DIEN BIEN PHU
Decisive battle of French Indochina in 1954

"Leave your stuff in the car. We'll be gone for only two days, so don't haul everything," I called over the car radio to my team. We are at the border of Lao PDR, where the northern parts of two Southeast Asian countries meet. Only two hours away, in Luang Namtha Laos bordering China's Yunnan province, CERS has been conducting studies of wildlife for several years. Now we want to have a look across the other border - that with Vietnam.

Today's political calm and buzzing border trade do not reflect the turbulent history of this corner where three countries meet. From six decades ago, in the early 1950s, right up until forty years ago in the late 1970s, the area was a hotspot for confrontation. Battles and wars have been fought here. One-time allies would later become enemies. To weave through the geopolitical complexities would require not only scholarly forensic study of history, but also consideration of the differing views of the same events, depending on which side of the fence each historian sat.

I had been longing to visit Dien Bien Phu for decades. The interest stemmed from my college days in America during the Vietnam War. As a young journalism and art student, our activities on campus were much affected by the anti-war sentiment which permeated all colleges in the late 1960s to the early 1970s. I was no exception, and was caught up in those movements. The Vietnam War, which America officially entered in 1964, was largely a continuation of the French-Indochina War. When the French left Vietnam, America filled the vacuum, supporting the South Vietnam regime for two more decades until it fell to the North, thus unifying the entire country.

Dien Bien Phu however, was the decisive battle that triggered the final retreat of the French colonialists from Indochina. The battle started toward the end of 1953 and finished in May 1954. The modern and superior forces of the French were routed and completely annihilated within one major battle that lasted 57 days, one of the longest battles in military history. Among Vietnamese historians, their publications compared the battle with those of the Three Kingdoms in China during the Third Century AD, claiming that it surpassed those in its accomplishment.

I have read many books regarding this battle, written from the viewpoint of the Vietnamese and of the French, who were both active participants, and that of the American's, who supported fully the French endeavor in the air as well as in military supplies, as well as the Chinese perspective, since they were deeply involved with support and execution of the battle,. The French

Uncle Ho & Giap in planning /
討論中的胡志民和武元甲將軍
Guide explaining French Army digging in /
導遊講解法軍的困境

Assembling tank while flight landing /
飛機降落時集結坦克車
Buffalo supply chain / 水牛運輸鏈
General Wei & Chen with Ho Chi-minh /
韋國清將軍和胡志民

forces were just newly relieved from World War II, of which they considered themselves the winner. Whereas, in my understanding, theirs was only a collateral success, by and large reliant on US military might, which defeated both the Nazi and the Japanese invaders in two respective theaters of war.

As for Dien Bien Phu, both the Vietnamese and Chinese views changed drastically after events led the two former allies into war against each other in the late 1970s. But one point is clear. This no doubt points to the deep involvement of Chinese on the frontline. Even in pamphlets that I got at the Vietnamese museum at Dien Bien Phu, published in 2010 both in English and Chinese, there is admission that the strategic plan was "approved by the military advisors of China".

The change of military tactics from a "quick and strong penetration" offensive to one that was a "protracted" maneuver falls fully in line with what Mao Zedong had defined for China's guerilla warfare, which ultimately took the entire country by storm. While it is unclear who made the call on this strategy, the Chinese lead advisor, General Wei Guoqing, a battle-proven military commander, had led the Chinese push for such a military decision. The group of Chinese advisors included some of China's most seasoned generals, like Chen Geng and Luo Guibo.

However, General Vo Nguyen Giap's 1960 book on Dien Bien Phu, published in Chinese in Hanoi, makes absolutely no mention of any Chinese involvement, except that a cache of artillery arrived from China to the front only after the battle was over. From his account, it can be seen early on that General Giap had the intention to assign full credit for the success at Dien Bien Phu strictly to the Vietnamese, and above all, to himself as commander-in-chief. But somehow within a few short years, his account has changed somewhat. On May 7, 1964, General Giap wrote in Vietnam's newspaper to commemorate the tenth anniversary of the Dien Bien Phu victory. "After 1950, China's revolution has succeeded. Our army and people had the condition to learn from the PLA their valuable experience and Chairman Mao's military thoughts. This helped greatly our army quiet development and provided success for our army, especially during 1953 to 1954 and during the battle of Dien Bien Phu.....

Despite this, in much later years, General Giap led a Vietnamese delegation to Beijing in 1992 and met with the wife of General Wei Guoqing. When asked at a banquet by her about his impression of General Wei, Giap thought for a moment and answered, "we get along very well, and have good feelings about each other. He has very stern determination about the revolution."

What is interesting is that both China and Vietnam underplay the role the Chinese military played in the battle of Dien Bien Phu, even to this day. Fortunately, a few first-person accounts of involvement from the Chinese side in the frontlines survived. We must also remember that the Chinese involvement was during the early years of the PRC when it had barely settled down after a drawn-out war on the Korean Peninsula. There is little doubt that the 105mm Howitzer and M-series anti-aircraft gun which was crucial in the siege of Dien Bien Phu must be sent over from China, captured during the Civil War and the Korean War. General Giap mentioned in his account that

China agreed to send over 7,400 rounds of 105mm artillery, all they had, to support the effort at the front, but the ammunition arrived two weeks too late, after the battle had ended with complete victory of the Vietnamese.

At the time, the entire military strategy in Vietnam was borrowed from the experience of the Chinese, including how to expand the army. Many Vietnamese military and political leaders were trained in China at one time or another. All the military supplies, be they from the Soviet Union or China, had to come through Yunnan or Guangxi to reach Vietnam. Not only did the operators of heavy artillery have to be trained by the Chinese, much of such equipment was often even manned by Chinese volunteers.

Many of the large bicycle corps, which was crucial in providing supplies behind the frontlines, were reinforced and donated by China. It would require a stretch of imagination to propose that French-made bicycles from Hanoi could be made available for use in those early days for such support. In fact, a two-volume book published in China in 1965 included first-person accounts of soldiers involved in the battle of Dien Bien Phu, has a chapter devoted to the bicycle transport corps, describing in great detail how the bikes were reconstructed and the caravan formed, the five-person per bicycle team, difficulties it encountered, and how it managed to provide support to the front.

But my trip was not to determine the role China played in Dien Bien Phu. That should be left to military historians. I was intent on making a "pilgrimage" to this famous battle ground, the site of the beginning of the end of European colonialism in Asia, to see it on the ground. A regular bus takes people crossing the border to the city, just an hour away. We arrived at the border just in time to catch the very last bus of the day. Checking into a hotel, there were seven of us.

The following morning, we first went to the museum that memorializes, or immortalizes, the Battle of Dien Bien Phu. It was this battle that defined the spirit of the North Vietnamese Army, who realized that overwhelming adversaries could be overcome. It also marked the determination of liberating the entire country as a national goal, thus leading to continuation of the struggle for two more decades until the ultimate goal was accomplished.

Though early in the morning, a group of elderly Vietnamese tourists were already inside the museum with a museum guide. A mock-up display of a battlefield war room and much of the artillery of the era were exhibited. The besieged French soldiers were featured in miserable and at times drunken states. The Vietnamese, of course, were portrayed in heroic maneuvers, firing their field guns. There were numerous maps to explain the forward movement of troops, as well as the demolition of each stronghold of the enemy.

Pictures as well as displays focused much on the peasant supply chain behind the front, especially the use of mules and bicycles as transport. Waste bottles of wine and liquor depicted the low morale of the French Army.

French with grim face / 沮喪的法國人

Display of French artillery / 法軍的軍火

Reinforced bicycle / 加強版的自行車

In contrast, a make-shift field hospital of the Vietnamese shows the highly organized support of the army behind the front lines, while soldiers in rather immaculate uniforms fire from battle trenches. The exhibit ends with two Vietnamese soldiers raising the single star red flag on top of the final highland bunker, and a picture of a young General Giap receiving political delegates of the Communist Party at the conquered site. Of course, there are also numerous pictures to show the defeated French commanders and their soldiers surrendering. It would indeed be a humiliating place for French tourists to visit today.

Next we visited the Cemetery of Revolutionary Heroes. There I saw that many of the tomb stones had fresh bouquets of flowers offered recently. I was surprised to see a young Vietnamese lady in jeans offering flowers at the altar. Sitting on the side was a middle- aged foreigner with an impressive upturned waxed moustache. Dr. Bleisch, who was among our group, started a conversation with this gentleman. It turned out that he was a Canadian member of the French Foreign Legion, the famed corps of mercenary soldiers fighting for France. He too was in Dien Bien Phu to pay tribute to the war dead, as well as retracing the footsteps of his predecessors. Later in the day, we visited the field command headquarters of General Giap, some distance out of town.

After our visit to the cemetery, we went up the neighboring hill, the actual site of the battlefield of the 57-day siege of the French at Dien Bien Phu. At the bottom of the battlefield was a line-up of French artillery, including tanks, armored vehicles, and cannons. Many of these had been partly destroyed during the battle.

As I left Dien Bien Phu on the last bus back to the Lao border, some thoughts went through my mind. I imagined future archaeologists scavenging the grounds, tunnels and trenches may someday come up with a cache of decades-old vintage French superior wine and champagne, hidden by the French to celebrate their final victory, which never came.

One may wonder why little mention and analysis are given to French General Navarre or the US involvement of support from the air and in the background. This is because of my belief in Sun Tzu's The Art of War. An arrogant army will always be defeated. Unfortunately, today we are still seeing countries falling into this same trap, waiting to be humbled.

To fight a battle or a war, you need strategy as well as tactics. But for a country, it also require a long term vision. Neighbors should recognize that geopolitical antics are only short term, whereas neighbors will not physically move away and must be reckoned with. Other distant "friends" may side with you for the time being, but once their political agenda or priority changes, they would certainly move away. It is best to live peacefully and enrich each other with stability.

In the case of Dien Bien Phu, two neighbors joined hands and fought off a faraway intruding colonial "power". This would continue into the next two decades until final victory against yet another even more formidable "power". For this alone, the battle of Dien Bien Phu should serve as an example for many nations with land or sea borders with each other, to have a united front against far-off enemies or "friends", rather than in collision course with each other.

奠邊府

一九五四年法國印度支那的決戰

「把你的東西留在車上。我們只會去兩天,不要拖任何東西!」我透過車上的無線電跟隊員說。我們正在寮國的邊界,正是兩個東南亞國家北部的交界處。琅南塔離中國雲南只有兩個鐘頭的距離,探險學會在邊境研究野生動物已經好多年了。現在我們想要跨過境去看看,去越南。

現在這裡政治平靜,邊境貿易也熱絡,似乎看不出這三個國家交界處曾經動盪的歷史。六十年前,一九五零年代初期一直到四十年前,也就是一九七零年代的後期,這裡可說是衝突的熱點。戰爭曾在這裡開打,過去的盟友後來變成敵人。要了解地緣政治的複雜性不僅需要從學術的角度對歷史的剖析,同時還需要考慮同一事件不同角度的觀點,歷史學家究竟是站在哪邊去看這件事的。

幾十年來我一直很想去奠邊府看看。這興趣跟我在美國讀大學的時候正在打越戰有關。當時我是新聞系和藝術系的學生,校園裡充斥著反戰的氛圍,這股情緒從一九六零年代後期一直維持到一九七零年代初。我當然也不例外,參與了這場運動。美國在一九六四年正式加入越戰,有很大的原因跟法國印度支那的戰役有關。當法國離開越南時美國填補了這個空缺,支持南越政權長達二十幾年,直到被北越擊敗後,越南才得以統一。

105mm Howitzer / 105 釐米 Howitzer
Attack on A1 strong hold / 攻擊 A1 據點
French consoling with wine / 法軍藉酒消愁

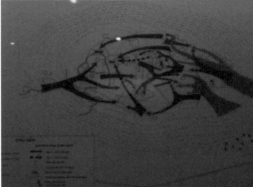

奠邊府的決戰最後讓法國殖民主義者從印度支那撤退。那場戰爭從一九五三年底開打直到一九五四年五月結束。法國現代化的優勢軍力在一場歷時五十七天的決戰中被殲滅，這是軍事史上最長的戰役之一。越南的史學家和他們發表的刊物把這場戰役跟西元三世紀時中國古代的三國之戰做比較，聲稱這場戰役的成就遠遠超越歷史上的三國之戰。

我閱讀過好幾本關於這場戰役的書，不只有從法國和越南兩方參戰者的角度寫的，還有美國的角度。美方曾全力支援法國空軍，也提供軍事物資。我也讀過從中國視角寫的，因為中方的介入也很深，不管是扮演支援或是執行的角色。當時法軍才剛結束二戰，自認為是戰勝者。但是以我的了解，他們是附隨依靠美國強大的軍力贏的，美軍可是真正擊敗過納粹和日本的侵略。

但是關於奠邊府，中國和越南因為一九七零年後期發生過一些衝突，因此看法變得徹底不同，昔日的盟友成為後來的敵人。但是有一點是清楚的，中國在前線的涉入甚深。就連我在奠邊府的越南博物館拿到的中英文對照小冊子（二零一零出版）都承認這場

Vietnamese field hospital / 越軍的戰地醫院
Soldiers in trenches ready to attack / 在壕溝裡的軍人準備進攻
Ultimate victory on top bunker / 站在地堡上慶祝勝利

戰略規劃是經過中國軍事顧問所「批准」的。

戰略從「迅速而有力的打擊」轉換成「持久戰」，毛澤東正是如此定義共產黨的游擊戰，他最後也是靠著這樣的戰略席捲整個中國。雖然無法確認到底是誰決定採取這個戰略的，但是這位身經百戰的軍事顧問主席韋國清將軍，的確曾經帶領著中國向這個軍事決策推進。這群中國顧問還包括一些最有經驗的將軍，像是陳賡和羅貴波。

然而，武元甲將軍一九六零年在河內，曾以中文出版關於奠邊府的書，他的書中完全沒有提到中國的參與，除了說到在戰爭結束後中國送了一批砲彈到前線以外。從他的描述，可以看出他想要將戰勝的功勞全部歸給越南，最重要的是歸功於當時身為總司令的自己。但是幾年後他的說法變了。一九六四年五月七日，武元甲將軍在越南報紙發表紀念奠邊府戰勝十周年的文章：「一九五零年之後，中國成功地革命。我們的軍隊和人民剛好有條件學習人民解放軍寶貴的經驗和毛主席的軍事思想。這對我們軍隊的發展有很大的幫助，尤其是在一九五三到五四年的奠邊府戰役。」

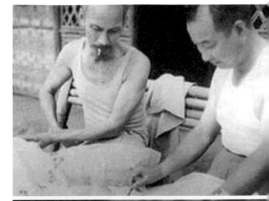

General Chen Geng with Ho Chi-minh / 陳賡將軍和胡志民
A jubilant General Giap upon victory / 戰勝後欣喜的武元甲將軍
French surrendering / 法軍投降

有趣的是，直到今天不管是中國還是越南都低估了中國軍方在奠邊府戰役中所扮演的角色。所幸那些曾在前線參與過戰役的中國軍人，他們親生經歷的故事被保留了下來。必須要記得的是，當時中華人民共和國才建國沒幾年，冗長的韓戰才剛結束。毫無疑問，那決定勝負的關鍵－ 105 釐米 Howitzer 和 M 系列的高射炮肯定是從中國送過去的，那些都是從中國內戰和韓戰中搜刮來的武器。武元甲將軍回憶，中國同意送七千四百多發 105 釐米的砲彈來支援前線，但是彈藥卻晚了兩個禮拜才送到，那時戰爭已經結束，越南軍贏了。

當時越南採用的整套軍事策略和思想都是借用中國的經驗，包括如何擴軍。許多越南的軍人和政治領袖都曾經在中國受過訓練。所有的軍事物資不管是從蘇聯還是中國運送過來，一定都要經過雲南或是廣西才能抵達越南。不僅運作重型火砲的人員必須由中方訓練，甚至許多設備還是由中國的志願者所操作的。

很多對前線提供補給至關重要自行車大隊，也都是中國援助和捐贈的。很難想像當時在河內法國人製造的自行車有多少可以派上用場。一九六五年有一套兩冊在中國出版的書,由當時參與奠邊府戰役的中國志願軍人自行述說當時的情況,裡面自行車運輸大隊就佔了一個章節,詳細記載了自行車要怎麼改裝,並由五個人組成一個自行車運輸隊,以及如何克服所遇到的困難好支援前線。

不過我這趟不是要去判定中國在奠邊府所扮演的角色,那應該留給軍事歷史學家去做。我只是想去這個有名的戰場「朝聖」,實地觀察歐洲殖民主義在亞洲被終結的開始。那裡有公車可以載乘客跨過邊境進城,只需要一個鐘頭。我們抵達邊境的時候剛好搭上最後一班公車往奠邊府。我們一共有七個人住進飯店。

隔天早上我們先去紀念,也或者是歌頌奠邊府戰役的博物館。這場仗彰顯了北越軍隊的精神,他們證明了再強大的對手也是可以被征服的。解放整個國家的決心是全國一致的目標,為此持續奮鬥了二十多年,一直堅持到最終目標實現。

雖然是一大早,但是已經有導覽員領著一組年長的越南觀光客在館內參觀了。展覽室裡有一間模擬的作戰情報室與當時所用的軍火。法軍被圍攻時的狼狽,和喝醉的樣子也是其中的展覽之一。越南人則是發射他們的野戰砲,被形塑的很英勇。有多張地圖說明越軍的行動,以及他們是怎麼攻陷敵軍的據點的。

照片和陳列特別突顯在後方的農民支援前線的補給鏈,尤其是用來運輸的馬騾和自行車。葡萄酒和烈酒的空瓶描繪法軍的士氣低落。相反的,越軍臨時搭建的戰地醫院顯示軍隊非常有組織地支援前線,即使是在壕溝裡開槍的越軍,身上的制服仍然表現得相當整潔。展覽以兩位越軍在高地的堡壘插起一面只有一顆紅星的旗子，以及一張年輕的武元甲將軍在戰勝的地點接受共產黨政治代表的照片作為結束。當然展覽裡還有很多張被擊敗的法國指揮官及投降士兵的照片。對於今天來參觀的法國遊客來說，這裡的確是個羞辱的地方。

接下來我們參觀了革命英雄的墓園。我看到許多墓碑前都有最近才獻上的鮮花。很驚訝地看到年輕的越南女子穿著牛仔褲也來獻花。有一位鬍鬚上了蠟並且兩端向上捲翹的中年外國人坐在一旁，畢博士主動找他聊天。原來這位加拿大人曾經效力於那個知名的法國僱傭軍團。他是來向在戰役中喪命的人致敬的，同時也回溯前輩曾走過的腳步。之後我們前去離城裡有點遠的地方參觀武元甲將軍的戰情室。

參觀完墓園後我們走上旁邊的山丘，那是奠邊府戰役裡圍攻法軍長達五十七天的地方。戰場的盡頭擺出法國大砲的陣容，有坦克車、裝甲車和大砲。其中許多武器在戰役中毀損了一部分。

Cemetery mausoleum / 陵墓

Offering at grave / 墓前獻花

當我搭上最後一班公車離開奠邊府，來到寮國邊界時，腦海裡浮現了一些念頭。我想像未來有一天當考古學家挖掘這塊戰場、坑道和戰壕的時候，或許會發現被藏起來的陳年法國上等葡萄酒和香檳，等著慶祝法軍勝利時享用，只是那場勝利最終沒有到來。

也許有人會好奇為什麼幾乎沒提到或是分析法國納瓦拉將軍抑是美國從空中或是地面上的援助。是因為我相信《孫子兵法》－驕兵必敗。很不幸的，直到今天我們還是會看到一些國家陷入同樣的陷阱，他們只是等著被教訓而已。

要打一場戰，你需要策略和戰術。而對一個國家來說更需要有遠見。互鄰者必須要認清地緣政治的衝突只是短暫的，沒有國家會因衝突而搬走，你必須跟他們打交道。遠方的「朋友」這時或許會站在你這邊，但是一旦政治議題或是優先順序改變的話，他們肯定會離開。最好是跟鄰居們和平相處，才能讓彼此安定的存活著。

奠邊府這案例，兩個鄰居聯手打敗來自遠方侵略者，一個殖民「強權」。這狀況後來持續了二十幾年，再一次打敗另一個更難對付的「強權」。許多國家的陸地或海洋的邊境緊鄰其他國家，奠邊府戰役給了他們很好的示範，聯合鄰居一起作戰對付遠來的敵人或是所謂一時的「友人」，而不是製造互相的衝突。

Destroyed artillery / 被摧毀的軍火

巴拉巴克，天堂還是地獄？

BALABAC, PARADISE OR HELL

Balabac, Palawan – December 10, 2018

BALABAC, PARADISE OR HELL
A land of both

Thirty-three-year old fisherman Cornelio Bonete was out looking for crab along a stretch of the mangrove not far from Balabac, a small island town off the southernmost tip of Palawan in the Philippines. Bonete had been conducting such activities since childhood, a way to supplement his family's diet if the crab he caught were small, and to supplement his income by sale in the market if the catch were big. On the night of November 27, however, there were neither big or small crab. Bonete did not return home.

The following day, family members went to his favorite spot and searched. His mutilated body was found on the shore of Sitio Bual. The victim's right arm and left foot were missing. The police and coastguard were quickly alerted and summoned to the scene. Checking the carcass, it was determined that Bonete was killed by a Saltwater Crocodile, one of the giant amphibious reptiles that frequented the neighborhood estuary, where the waters of the river and the sea mingle.

By December 1, a team of croc experts were called in from the provincial capital of Puerto Princesa (PPS). A cow was slaughtered and raw meat used as bait. Soon a 15-foot crocodile weighing 500 kilos was entrapped and restrained. It was transported to PPS for observation and a round of *"gastrointestinal decontamination"*, an act of pumping the stomach of the animal to flush out its content for inspection. Later, the *"flushing"* procedure was called off, citing that the animal, now nicknamed *"Singko"*, referring to the location it was captured, might become too stressed and die. Besides, other evidence already provided enough proof that the caught croc was the culprit in the death of Bonete.

Critics, especially some environmentalists, cited the conflict between man and beast as being the result of habitat destruction, the decrease of the animal's habitat caused by cutting down the coastal mangrove forests. Such mangrove is crucial for the crocodile to subsist on its natural prey. Failing that, the carnivore would go for human.

This was the third or fourth case of crocodile attack on humans within the last two years; each time the victim was killed or severely injured. Before that, men and croc seemed to live peacefully next to each other. The last time such brutality, or worse, happened around here was when a German was kidnapped from his yacht by the Abu Sayyaf terrorist group and beheaded before ransom could arrive. Such headline-catching news had already stopped any tourist or vacationer from setting foot on this remote island, despite that the croc attacks only started quite recently, and the beheading was just over a year ago.

Land delivery of "Singko" / 陸上運輸「Singko」

Shipping "Singko" to PPS / 運送「Singko」到公主港

Giant-Crocodile / 巨大的鱷魚

I, however, was not deterred. Not because of bravery or stupidity, but because my journalistic instinct told me that most news is usually exaggerated and dramatized, in order to get attention, not unlike how I chose the crocodile story to start off this article. Let alone, I am not traveling in a posh yacht that attracts undue attention, and thus the ransom seeking terrorists. A good friend Vince Perez, former Secretary of Energy for the Philippines and past WWF Chairman, told me how beautiful and pristine the area was. He, however, arrived in a helicopter by air, with full security detail.

Balabac, at the southernmost tip of Palawan in the Philippines, seems to embrace both heaven and hell, famed as a tropical island paradise with turquoise atolls, coral reefs, pearl culture, sea turtles, but also notorious as a land of pirates, kidnappings, Muslim extremists, and more lately even with headlines of killer crocodile. Paradise, a town in northern California, could turn from its heavenly namesake to hell overnight. It was only a month ago when wild fire ravaged the Californian town, leaving many dead, hundreds unaccounted for, and almost 30,000 people evacuated. Just so, Balabac can also be transformed from hell to paradise, in fact, back and forth, depending on what, where and when we choose to focus our attention.

I choose to believe that the bad news is exceptional and selective, whereas the good news is the norm. That is what we went for, and certainly we were rewarded in plenty. For me, it is not unlike a quiet town in America suddenly shot to national and international fame because of a once-in-a-century headline-catching mass shooting. In contrast, Everest and K2 are mountaineer killers year after year, but there is no shortage of climbers attempting to reach the summit.

It was such spirit that drove me to lead a small team to scout out the real situation in Balabac, an island I have wanted to visit since first arriving in Palawan over three years ago. The 580 square kilometer island is somewhat larger than Lantao in Hong Kong, and off the main island of Palawan. Even electricity is off the grid, depending on a large generator to provide for the needs of the town, but only from 2pm to 6am every day. As a crow flies, it is less than 50 kilometers from the northern islands of Sabah in Malaysia.

Nonetheless, warnings are to be taken seriously and some precaution had to be made, as with all exploration expeditions. With us were CQ Robin and CQ Suyuer. CQ is my term for Security. Both were from the intelligence service of Palawan. Both were Muslims originally from the islands around Balabac. They ought to know if there were danger looming, as they were responsible for our safety.

Five hours by car took us from Puerto Princesa to Rio Tuba in Bataraza where the main pier is at the south tip of Palawan. There a charter ferry boat, capable of taking 80 passengers, was sitting in wait for us five, in addition to the two CQs. It was already late afternoon and right before sunset, so we quickly loaded our gear and food onto the boat and set off. As the sun set, we passed several beautiful islands on both sides, but did not stop. Three hours later in the dark, after going through some choppy sea, we arrived inside the estuary bay of Balabac. By then only some dim lights lit the small town by the water.

With a motor-tricycle making two trips, all of us arrived at a hillside lodge with two spartan, but very clean, rooms. First surprise; the rooms came with air-conditioners, and they worked. Toilet was basic, and a bucket worked as shower. As with most remote islands, if you have running water off a tap, that's considered a luxury. Second surprise; our rooms had pictures of the Virgin Mary and Christian emblems on the wall, although this

Muslim ladies in rain / 雨中的穆斯林女士們
Scorpion in rain / 雨中的蠍子

is known to be a Muslim area. A simple dinner was soon cooked and consumed, and everyone felt ready for the days ahead. That night, I heard my first live-story about killer crocodiles looming in the dark.

The next morning, it rained hard, unusual for this late in the season. We went early to register with the local police, and the policewoman had our pictures and passports taken for record. She even posed with us for a group portrait. We also met Toto, the Balabac Councilor who arranged all our island-hopping itinerary. Across from the police station is perhaps the only decent café in town, next to the main pier. Naturally we had our breakfast there, while it was pouring outside.

As the space under the house became like a stream, I saw a scorpion crawling out into the street. Such a tiny pest can be quite nasty, comparable to the killer croc, though inflicting a slower but perhaps more painful injury, at times fatal. As the rain stopped, I nosed around town and saw quite a few young and old ladies in partial veil. I managed to see a couple of older women with even a full veil.

One of the fully-veiled women I met was Amina. She had previously been a Christian, and turned Muslim after marrying her husband almost thirty years ago. Now she says Islam is the true religion. Her husband Omar is

Fully-veiled Amina / 穿戴全面紗的 Amina   Amina in Omar's shadow / 在 Omar 影子後的 Amina

the local Imam who presides over the service in the mosque. She kept offering to show me the almost finished new mosque, but I declined, as I had just come from a visit there. Momentarily her husband walked up and we had a good chat. They would love to go on the pilgrimage, but going to Mecca is prohibitively expensive, costing around 80,000 peso, or over 12K USD. However, our CQ Robin was already addressed as Haji, an honor bestowed on those who have visited Mecca.

What seemed unusual in Balabac is that the Christians live very peacefully among the Muslim majority. Our informants said the town is about 90 percent Muslim, but the red-brick church is relatively grand and new, with a tall bell tower. It is literally a few steps away from the new mosque, just around the corner. The minaret seemed to stand higher with its moon and star insignia. Apparently, that may be good enough for the Muslims. While in town, folks were celebrating a pre-Christmas Christian festival, and everything seem joyous and festive, though basic compared to more populated cities.

There is little information available on the smaller islands, some forty or so, near Balabac. We headed straight for Onuk, the jewel among them. The Councilor, Toto, who co-owns the island, had made arrangements for us to stay two nights at a lodge, built on top of a 100-meter jetty protruding into the sandbar. As our boat sailed for an hour through calm and rough sea, we approached Onuk and right away I knew we had chosen the right spot to spend our time - a truly off-the-grid enclave.

One account called the water "sapphire blue". Another nature worshipper described it as emerald, crystal, and deep blue. It has only caught the attention of off-the-beat travelers within the last couple years. A photographer from Manila caught a scene with a rainbow that landed him an award from the National Geographic. One blogger called it "island Paradise", another said "breathtaking", while two others described it as "Undiscovered Paradise," "Hidden Gem" and "The Most Beautiful Spot in the Philippines". And these are Filipinos who had frequented many pristine islands within their country.

The entire island with coconut trees, but no regular residents, is about 300-meters long and half that in width. Thus, walking around the entire atoll may take only fifteen to twenty minutes. Perhaps the word, boondocks, which came from Tagalog, is quite fitting, meaning the back and beyond. But then, Onuk is exceptionally beautiful to be called such.

It is rare that I idle the day away, but in this case the better part of two days were filled with almost a single preoccupation. As the tide came in, so did dark shadows, bobbing up and down along with the surf, just below the surface. These are the Green Sea Turtles, swimming near to shore to forage on the seaweed hugging the bottom. As I watched from a deck on the jetty, some came as close as five meters from where I stood.

I would wait patiently until the turtle would pop up to the surface for a breath of fresh air, which generally happened every five to ten minutes. Just as the head popped up, my camera would click - another shot taken, while hoping the auto-focus would freeze the turtle in sharp focus. I could follow that routine all day long without feeling tired. The same turtles would come in at night to the beach, to lay eggs before returning to the sea. When the tide receded and the turtles were out at sea, I would then take to the beach to swim or snorkel a bit. When lying around, I contemplated the Old Man and the Sea Turtle.

Two days on Onuk and another day at Balabac passed by quickly, and we were soon on our way back to our base by the Maoyon River an hour north of PPS. But before that, we visited several more islands, most hosting a small community. One such village, Mantangule, stood out. Barely an hour from the main island and Rio Tuba, it is perhaps the largest island community among the group. Most families engaged in fishing and farming of seaweed. The water was crystal clear and many sheds with fish nets below were built over the water slightly off shore, reachable by narrow plank-ways.

We visited one such shed with fish and lobster nets below deck. The two types of lobster caught here are dark green and pale green, the latter being considered "Class One." The catch is not sold to the Philippines side, but instead to Malaysia, which apparently provides higher returns. We bought several of each type, the former at 2300 peso per kilo and the latter 5000p. A spotted garoupa weighing almost three kilos went for 1250p (around USD25), a fraction of what it would cost in Hong Kong.

At Mantangule, I was also fascinated by a make-shift school where locals teach Arabic to little kids during after-school hours. Most people living among these islands also speak Malay, and their boats, both large outriggers and the faster speed boats, take on the shape and style of those from Malaysia, rather than resembling those in Palawan.

As our team turned back on our long drive home, I kept pondering the killer crocodile story. It was in 1985 when I was exploring the entire Yangtze River for the National Geographic. I stopped by Wuhu to find out about the Yangtze Alligator, an endangered species. It was then that I found out that along the coast of southern China there used to be Saltwater Crocodile as well. But long since, the killer croc has become extinct in China.

During the Tang Dynasty, Han Yu (768-824AD), a scholar and member of the court literati, was exiled and banished to become governor of Chiu Zhou, an ancient town adjacent to today's Swatow port in northern Guangdong province. At the time, crocodile infested the estuary waters, and both livestock and humans were regular victims. Han wrote an edict and burnt it as an offering to heaven. In it, he ordered the crocodile to move south and away from the populated area, warning that otherwise he would organize the locals to eradicate them. Apparently, this threat worked and, from then on, the menace of the crocodile was eliminated, as they moved south for some six hundred kilometers.

Suddenly I recalled at the small and beautiful island of Kenderamen, we interviewed 49-years-old Ben Jahuji whose family was there seasonally to harvest seaweed, to be collected and sold to Japan.

He recounted recently seeing a huge crocodile swimming near their beach. "The animal is very very big, over fifteen feet long. His body very wide, just like a big drum," described Ben. This reminded me of another historic story about the crocodile in China.

This story circulated that since the time of Spring and Autumn era, some 3,000 years ago, Chinese had been choosing crocodile hide to make the best battle drums, the beating of which was a signal for the army to advance and attack. For retreat or calling off fighting when darkness approaches, a gong would be sounded. As the crocodile is an amphibious, the hide has the best sound retention quality, be it rain or shine, whereas cow hide could not produce the same quality sound and resonance in a battlefield when it rained.

Perhaps because the Chinese fought too many battles throughout the centuries, the crocodile went extinct in China. However, for ladies who enjoy sporting a crocodile handbag, maybe they should know that such bags will weather nicely, looking just as elegant during a shiny or rainy day.

My visit to Balabac was surely like visiting paradise on a sunny day, until another episode of disaster. Then, for the victims, hell it may become once again.

Muslim girls learning Arabic / 學習阿拉伯語的穆斯林女孩們

巴拉巴克，天堂還是地獄？

是天堂也是地獄

三十三歲的漁夫 Comelio Bonete 沿著一段很長的紅樹林抓螃蟹，這裡離巴拉巴克不遠，巴拉巴克是菲律賓巴拉望最南方的離島小鎮。Bonete 從小就會抓螃蟹，抓到小隻的就幫家人加菜，抓到大隻的就拿到市場賣，貼補家用。十一月二十七日 那天，大隻或小隻的螃蟹都沒有捕到，Bonete 沒有回到家。

隔天，家人到他平常喜歡去的地方找他。在 Sitio Bual 岸邊找到他被肢解的屍體。他的右手和左腳都不見了。當地的警察和海岸警衛隊很快地趕到現場。查看屍體後，確定 Bonete 是被鹹水鱷魚殺害，這種巨型兩棲爬行動物經常在附近淡水和海水交會的河口出沒。

十二月一日，公主港省會的鱷魚專家們趕到現場，他們殺了一頭牛當作誘餌，不久就抓到一隻重達五百公斤的鱷魚。鱷魚被送到公主港觀察並預計進行「腸胃清洗」，看腸胃裡有什麼東西。但是後來取消了這道手續，外號 Singko 的鱷魚，有可能身體會承受不住；名字 Singko 是牠起自被捕獲的地方。其他的證據就足以證明牠就是殺害 Bonete 的兇手。

評論者，尤其是環保人士說這場人類與動物的衝突正是因為牠們棲息的沿岸紅樹林被破壞。這片紅樹林是鱷魚賴以為生的地方，失去了紅樹林，鱷魚自然會找上人類算帳。

在過去的兩年裡這好像是第三還是第四起鱷魚攻擊人類的案件，受害者不是死了就是受重傷。但以前，人類和鱷魚好像可以和平共處的。之前這裡曾發生殘暴的事件，有個德國人在他的船上被 *Abu Sayyaf* 恐怖組織綁架，贖金還沒到，他就已經被砍頭了。這樣驚悚的新聞讓觀光客不敢踏上這個離島，鱷魚攻擊人類是最近的事，而砍頭事件則是一年多前發生的。

我，卻沒有止步。並不是因為特別勇敢或是愚蠢，而是我當記者的直覺告訴我新聞通常都會誇大，好吸引目光，就像我會選上鱷魚來開始這篇文章一樣。再加上我又不是搭豪華遊艇，不會吸引不需要的關注，像是要贖金的恐怖組織的青睞。我的好朋友 *Vince Perez* 是前菲律賓能源部長和世界自然基金會主席，他告訴我這裡有多麼的原始，有多漂亮。而他則是搭直升機來的，還帶著一隊保鑣。

巴拉巴克位於菲律賓 *Palawan* 巴拉望島（我稱它為「派來玩」）的最南方，似乎是個天堂也是個地獄，以熱帶小島的天藍色環礁、珊瑚礁、珍珠文化、海龜出名；但是島上的海盜、綁匪、穆斯林極端分子還有最近上新聞的鱷魚殺手更是惡名昭彰。「天堂」是加州北部的一個城鎮，一夕之間變成地獄。一場野火摧殘這個鎮，死傷慘重數百人下落不明，近三千人撤離家園。就像這樣，巴拉巴克也有可能從地獄變成天堂，或是從天堂變成地獄，那得要看我們把注意力放在哪裡，什麼時候關注。

我選擇相信負面的新聞是例外，是選擇性的，而正面新聞則是平靜普通的日常。這是我們來這裡的原因，無疑的我們收穫良多。對我來說這就像美國一個安靜的小鎮，因為百年一次的大規模槍擊事件上了新聞頭條，突然舉國甚至是世界知名。相反的，聖母峰和 *K2* 年復一年取走登山者的性命，但還是不乏登山者想要征服它們。

Looking out from Onuk island / 從 Onuk 島看出去
Sea turtle popping up / 海龜冒出頭
Sea turtle in turquoise water / 海龜在碧綠的海水中

隔絕的地方。小島的主人是 *Toto* 委員，安排我們在一家沙洲上的所謂旅店住宿兩個晚上，距離碼頭只有一百米。

有人形容這裡的水像「藍寶石藍」。崇拜自然的人說是祖母綠，既清透又深藍。過去這幾年才開始吸引一些非典型的菲律賓國內遊客。曾經有一位的馬尼拉攝影師在這裡拍了一張彩虹照，那張照片讓他贏得美國《國家地理雜誌》的獎項。有位部落客稱這裡為「小島天堂」，另一位則形容「美的令人窒息」，又有兩位說這裡是「未被發現的天堂」，「隱藏的寶石」，「菲律賓最美的地方」。這些描述都是出自於經常探訪原始島嶼的菲律賓人。

島上都是椰子樹，沒有長期的住民，大約三百公尺長，寬是長度的一半。走一圈環礁只需要十五到二十分鐘。也許可以用這個字「*boondocks* 偏遠地區」來形容，這個外語其實是菲律賓他加祿語。但 *Onuk* 除了偏遠卻又格外的美麗，「*Boondocks*」這詞用在她身上好像又不那麼完全貼切。

我很少閒暇度日，這兩天我都專注在一件事。當潮水進來時，一些黑影也跟著來，在水面下隨著海浪沉沉浮浮。這是綠蠵龜來覓食，它們游到岸邊找抓從海底長出的海草。我站在碼頭的陽台上看著這景象，有些綠蠵龜甚至離我站著的地方只有五公尺。

我很有耐心地等候海龜浮出水面換氣，通常五到十分鐘一次。當牠頭一冒出來，我的相機就會喀嚓一聲，又拍了一張，希望自動對焦會清晰地定格海龜。我可以整天都這樣過也不會覺得累。這些海龜夜晚會上岸產卵然後再回到海裡。當潮退時，海龜也跟著出海了，這時我會去海邊游泳或是浮潛一下。這種閒暇時刻讓我想到老人與海龜。

兩天在 Onuk，一天在巴拉巴克，這些時間都過得很快，我們又回到 Maoyon 河邊的基地，離公主港一個鐘頭。其間我們又去了幾個小島，這些小島上面有些小社區。有個叫 Mantangule 的村子很特別，離里奧圖巴及大島不到一個鐘頭，這個村落可能是這些小島上最大的社區。大多數人從事捕魚和採海藻的工作。海水清澈，許多掛著魚網的棚子都蓋在岸邊的水面上，木板步道可以走到。

我們去看了一個棚子，捕魚和捕龍蝦的魚網就掛在陽台下。這裡捕到的龍蝦有兩種，一種深綠色一種淺綠色，後者被視為「極品」。這些漁獲不是賣到菲律賓而是送往馬來西亞，很明顯的利潤比較好。我們各買了幾隻，深綠色一公斤二千三比索，淺綠色一公斤五千比索。一尾老鼠斑重達快三公斤只要一千二百五十比索，大約美金二十五元，還不到香港賣價的零頭呢。

在 Mantangule 當地人會在課後利用簡易搭建的教室來教小朋友阿

Drying fish at Mantangule / 在 Mantangule 曬魚干
Lobster galore / 好多龍蝦
Big garoupa / 大尾的石斑魚

Children play Chinese crab game / 孩童們玩遊戲
Muslim shopkeeper / 穆斯林店家

拉伯語，這讓我覺得很有意思。大部分住在這些小島的人都會說馬來語，他們的船，外伸樂架小艇和快艇的外型風格都很馬來西亞，不太像是巴拉望的。

當我們團隊在回程的路途上時，我不斷想到殺人鱷魚的故事。一九八五年當我還在美國《國家地理雜誌》工作時，我把長江從頭到尾都探索了一遍，並且在安徽蕪湖發現瀕臨絕種的淡水長江楊子鱷。那時我才知道原來中國南方沿岸也曾有鹹水的鱷魚出沒。但是那些殺人鱷魚早就在中國絕種了。

唐朝的御用文人韓愈（西元 768 – 824 年）曾經被流放到現在廣東省北部鄰近汕頭港的潮州古鎮。當時河口滿是鱷魚，使得牲畜和鄉民經常受害。於是他寫了〈祭鱷魚文〉燒給上天。他命令鱷魚們往南移，離開人口稠密的地區，如果不乖乖聽從的話，他就會下令將牠們消滅。這招似乎真的奏效，鱷魚不見了，牠們往南遷移了六百公里。

我突然想起那個很漂亮的 Kenderamen 小島，在那裏我們訪問了四十九歲的 Ben Jahuji，他和家人正好在島上採收海帶，準備賣到日本。他說最近看到一隻很大的鱷魚游過他們的海灘。「這隻真的真的很大，超過十五呎長。身體很寬，跟個大鼓一樣」，Ben 如此描述。這又讓我想到關於鱷魚在中國的另一個歷史故事。

Palawan authorities capture man-eating crocodile / 巴拉望當局捕獲吃人的鱷魚

Catching of crocodile / 捕捉鱷魚

大約三千年前的春秋時期，最好的戰鼓都是用鱷魚皮做成的。當戰鼓一響，就表示軍隊要開始向前進攻。若是要撤退或因為天黑了要停戰，則敲鑼示意。鱷魚是兩棲動物，不管是雨天或晴天牠的皮革發出來的聲音都是最好的，而牛皮在雨天的時候就沒有辦法在戰場上發出這樣好的聲音跟共鳴。

或許中國幾世紀以來打過太多仗了，所以在中國已經找不到鱷魚了。喜歡用鱷魚皮包的女士們都應該知道，這種包包不受天候的影響，不管是晴是雨，包包都一樣的優雅好看。

因為沒有任何的災難發生，所以我的巴拉巴克之旅就好像在晴天去了一趟天堂。而對於那些受害者來說，下一趟倘發生意外，這裡就如地獄一般。

再訪布拉格

CZECH MATE!
PRAGUE REVISITED

Prague, Czech Republic – July 20, 2019

Vstup na vě
Entrance

PANORAMATICKÁ VYHLÍ
PANORAMIC OBSERVATION

Prodej suvenýrů / Souvenir sho

CZECH MATE! PRAGUE REVISITED

Third day in Prague, 3pm. Weather has changed. Pouring outside and so I stopped by the business center of the hotel for help. All umbrellas checked out, so I wait patiently for someone to return to the hotel. Fifteen minutes or so, a gentleman comes in with a wet umbrella. The lady at the counter turns it over to me.

I only need to go a block, around the corner. In such a heavy downpour without waterproof shoes, it would be unwise to go any further. I was planning to visit the museum next to the Marriott on the day of my arrival, but failed to do so due to jetlag. Now that my closing keynote for the World Leading Schools Association is over, I am more relaxed and have caught up on my jetlag a bit.

At the small entrance to this somewhat unique theme museum a line has gathered. After all, where else can tourists go in the rain? I pay 270 czk for entry, receiving a symbolic 7 percent discount in respect of my being a senior. The long stairs up to a shining red star would seem an appropriate approach to a museum of modern art. In some sense, that is what it is. The Museum of Communism, which portrays the country's grim history under communist rule, is a part of modern art, albeit the art of propaganda and governing or, in the eyes of the creator of the museum, misgoverning.

The first few displays briefly describe the historic setting of the industrial revolution which led up to Marx and Engel's work on the Communist Manifesto, which in turn precipitated the Russian revolution, the birth of the Soviet Union, the leadership of Lenin, then Stalin, the 'dictatorship of the proletariat,' and ultimately the forming of the Eastern Bloc and the "communistization" of Czechoslovakia. The displays then go on; to the Prague Spring, the fall of the Berlin Wall, finally to arrive at today's Czech Republic.

Life, or non-life, under communism and a totalitarian regime behind the Iron Curtain is prominent in the exhibits. Models of a shop with meager merchandise, a barren school classroom with one student, an athlete's spartan dorm room, secret police and the horror of interrogation mechanics are but a few of the highlights.

At a loft souvenir shop, copies of propaganda posters are sold, and postcards containing smart quotes to mock the former system. Interestingly, posters of the era are far more expensive than the "smart" cards. Joining the crowd, I too purchase two sets of posters and one postcard.

Stairs up to museum / 通往博物館的階梯

Star with Marx statue / 馬克思雕像和星星

Sports display / 關於運動的展示

There were perhaps three ironies in the museum, at least during the time of my visit. The café looked as barren as the display of the communist era, and it was closed, during the busiest hours. Secondly, the museum shop stocked rather sparse items. Thirdly, the many short films of the past recounting the horror of communist rule used many older folks to provide evidence and personal stories, but the senior ticket discount was only paltry.

It would be far more balanced, believable and better appreciated if even just a tiny positive notion could be given to an era that, while it may have been evil and a failure, somehow lasted for over four decades. Among the horde of manipulators and collaborators, there must have been a few idealists within the system. Though now defunct and dismembered, it was once the driving force behind the efforts of an entire generation.

As Tripadvisor noted, "the front desk staff have perfectly captured the spirit of Communist service," a suitable addition to "it rains in Prague, and there is nowhere to hang a wet coat or umbrella." Perhaps anything left unattended may well revert to an old habit!

It may seem insensitive for someone like myself who hasn't lived under communism to make comments on the system and how it is presented. But neither has Glenn Spicker, the American businessman who created this museum. Rather it is based on his interest in history and politics, especially that of the eastern Bloc. But the dogmatic negativism and skewed interpretation is perhaps overly one-sided. The scientific talent that brought about the first satellite, Sputnik, in 1957 and the first cosmonaut in space in 1961 must have had some foundation as well, though

Communist era painting / 共產時代的繪畫
Display of secret police / 特務
Spartan classroom / 簡樸的教室

nurtured under a Communist regime.

If a similar communism museum were to be choreographed in China, it may come to show that its entrepreneurs today account for the second highest number of billionaires in the world, twice as many as in Germany. Furthermore, of the biggest banks in the world, China netted the top four spots, hardly a model for failure of the system. The 150 million tourists who left China and dutifully returned dutifully would suck fuel from the theory of a virtual "Berlin Wall" or "Bamboo Curtain". Of course, others could argue that China is not really a representation of communism, yet it is surely and firmly under the rule of the Communist Party.

As the rain stopped, so did my visit. I wanted to turn my mind to something more positive. Returning to my hotel, I read the Sunday papers, the Weekend Financial Times and USA Today, from two diverging continents, but with converging outlook. Each had on its front page an image from the historic first lunar landing with Astronaut Buzz Aldrin in the picture. A coincidence and corollary to my earlier thoughts regarding the Soviet's space program.

Entrance of Café Louvre / Louvre 咖啡館入口
Café Louvre interior / Louvre 咖啡館內部
Meal at Café / 在咖啡館內用餐

Next to that canal, just a short earshot from the Prague's Vltava River, is a small restaurant. Café Restaurant Marnice has a sign board outside the kitchen window facing the street. It is in Chinese, proclaiming that the restaurant was the location for a Chinese film shoot, Somewhere Only We Know, a romantic Chinese drama released in 2015. This is the only Chinese movie using Prague as theme and location set. Such distinction no doubt attracts more Chinese to the restaurant, with loads of selfies being taken next to the sign board.

No trip to such a colorful city as Prague can be considered complete without shopping. No shopping can be more colorful than the purchase of art supplies. I purchase a large amount of pastel and drawing pencils, all made by the famous Czech art supplies maker, Koh-I-Noor. From Pylones, another colorful shop, I purchase an artist's apron and an assortment of sundry products. Embossed hand-made paper, though expensive, now graces my stationary inventory.

My last purchase before leaving for the Prague train station is perhaps also worth mentioning. My most colorful, ten-year-old Mywalit, an Italian wallet, is becoming worn and a bit torn, so it is time to buy a replacement. There is a small Mywalit kiosk at the shopping center a block from the Marriott. I take a stroll over there.

Under the counter glass display is a 'Sale!' sign announcing 20% off. I choose a wallet costing 1800 czk (USD78) and ask for the discount. The young lady says only higher priced items receive 20%, whereas my wallet can only enjoy 10%, so my cost would be 1620 czk. She asks me to give her the 10% of 180 czk in cash first, then she will charge the difference of 1440 czk to my credit card.

While I am still wondering about the procedure, she already takes my credit card and enters 1620 czk into the card machine. I point out that, adding cash to card, I would have no discount left at all. She suddenly realizes her mistake and is compelled to return my cash. In that instant, I also realize her game … the 10% discount in cash would not be registered and she could have pocketed it. Unfortunately, her math did not work out, as she forgot to deduct my 10% discount.

I leave the shop thinking to myself that, after all, communism and capitalism are not that much different when it gets down to street level.

Discreet local wedding shot / 低調的婚紗照

搭了街頭電車去市中心吃晚餐，我不選那些看起來新潮豪華的，特別挑選了一家舊餐館。河畔邊的盧浮咖啡館創立於一九零二年。值得一提的是，這裡不僅環境古典還有個很大的撞球間，裡面有好幾張撞球檯，而這裡也是許多歷史名人不管是白天或是晚上都喜歡來的地方。知識分子、作家、科學家、藝術家和音樂家在二十世紀初都是這裡的常客。像是愛因斯坦和卡夫卡還有其他我比較不熟悉的捷克名人。據說愛因斯坦在布拉格的德國大學任教物理學的那一年就經常來這裡。

我帶了一本圖文小說《布拉格政變》準備餐後享用咖啡的時候閱讀，這本書部分是虛構的，部分卻真實的紀錄了戰後冷戰時期的維也納和布拉格。驚悚故事裡的間諜主角是英國情報單位 MI6 的一員，他臥底冒充為一位電影製作，與惡名昭彰的「劍橋五人組」的吉伯斯和費爾比有關。我可以想像，有一個神出鬼沒的人坐在盧浮咖啡館角落看報紙，但是他的眼角卻老是飄向陽台遠處的另一桌。

亞洲人尤其是中國觀光客已經走遍了歐洲各大城市，布拉格也不例外。這裡有許多旅行團，也有許多自由行的觀光客，但是亞洲人跟白種人比還是相對的少。儘管如此中國人還是會被注目。在最受歡迎的景點「查理大橋」，一對男女在眾目睽睽之下拍攝婚紗照。但同時我也看到一對當地的戀人低調的在橋墩邊拍婚紗照。

Chinese couple wedding shot / 中國新人拍婚紗照

Street of Prague / 布拉格街景
In front of film location restaurant /
電影場景裡的餐廳

Vltava 河邊有一家小餐館 *Mamice*，就位在運河旁。餐廳廚房的窗子對外擺著一塊木板，上面用中文寫著這是中國電影《有一個地方只有我們知道》的場景。這是唯一一部用布拉格做為主題和場景的中國電影。因此毫無疑問地吸了引許多中國遊客來用餐和跟這塊招牌自拍。

來到布拉格這個多采多姿的城市怎麼能不買買東西呢。有什麼會比藝術用品更多采多姿。我買了很多粉蠟筆、繪圖鉛筆，都是捷克當地出名的廠牌 *Koh-I-Noor* 的。在另一家有趣的店 *Pylones* 我買了藝術家圍裙還有各式各樣的小東西。壓紋的手工紙雖然貴，也被我收藏了。

前往布拉格火車站之前我又買了一個值得一提的東西。我的義大利製錢包已經用了十年了，磨損到需要買一個新的。離 *Marriott* 飯店一街區有個購物中心，裡面有一家「我的錢包」小店。

玻璃櫃下寫著「八折！」。我選了一個標價捷克幣一千八（美金七十八元）的皮夾，然後跟店員要折扣。年輕的女店員說只有高單價品才有八折，我選的只有九折，所以我需要付總共捷克幣一千六百二。她要我先付捷克幣一百八的現金，然後剩下的一千四百四十她會算在我的信用卡。

Night fall in Prague / 夜裡的布拉格

我還在想為什麼這麼複雜的時候，她已經拿走我的信用卡刷了一千六百二十。我跟她說那不是沒有折扣了嗎？她才發現她犯的錯誤似地，退我現金。後來，我想通了她的盤算，那十趴不會被記錄，她可以放進自己的口袋。很不幸的，她的數學不好，忘了把她要給我九折扣掉。

離開的時候我心想，在現實的街頭上，共產主義跟資本主義其實沒有多大的差別。

三個Ｂ開頭的城市
柏林、巴賽爾、布魯塞爾

The 3 B's, Berlin, Basel & Brussels

London – August 5, 2019

London – August 5, 2019

The 3 B's, Berlin, Basel & Brussels
and a few London historic hide-outs

I quietly retreat from the library and cross the hallway to the drawing room. After all, I won't look the part in shorts and boat shoes; rather distracting for the ladies working inside this Victorian-era library. Perhaps they would mistake me for a janitor or one of the repairmen working inside the Club. At the moment, there are three women in the library, all dressed properly and professionally.

Founded in 1883, this club has seen history, especially educated women's history, for almost one and a half centuries. This is the University Women's Club of London, at a hide-away corner of Mayfair. The dining room, library and drawing room are excellent venues for meetings, functions, and lectures, with almost exclusively female speakers. Much of the facilities, however, will be occupied this Sunday, for a wedding.

The 22 bedrooms are essentially for professional women members who live outside of London, but for convenience, can stay and spend a night or two here. Of these 22 rooms, only three rooms are en-suite. The rest have shared bathrooms. The elevator, called "lift" of course, barely fits three persons and still has a hand-pushed accordion-like metal gate behind the hinged door.

UWC's library / 女子大學俱樂部的圖書館

I am lucky to book into one of the three rooms. My bathroom, appropriately ancient, still has a pull-string light switch suspended from the ceiling, turning on and off with a loud "click." For the last five days since moving in, I have seen no other male guests, which should not be surprising as the Club only accepts female members. I get to use the Club as a member of the Helena May Club, a reciprocating Ladies Club in Hong Kong that long ago lifted the "ladies only" restriction.

The library is, however, of particular interest to me. It recalls the many meals I had at the Yale Club in New York, also with a wonderful library. For the last few days, I have often sat quietly on the old sofas of the library here, watching the fireplace, though without anything burning in it. The unusual heat wave of Europe and the UK these two summers foretells changes that will render fireplaces obsolete in the future, whereas air-conditioning may be installed, thus advancing global warming. What an irony!

When alone in a library, I always feel the ghosts of all the authors are there with me. Here both the floor and the sofas squeak as one walks or sits on them. It has a certain romance and ambience for a seasoned writer. Momentarily, my eyes turn to a wall shelf full of very old books. I walk over and browse carefully. On the slightly torn book ends, one book reads "Travels." I make an attempt to pull out this old volume. It refuses to budge. Perhaps no one has read it for a very long time and it somehow has gotten stuck.

A small brass button on a lower ledge catches my eyes. Curious as I always am, I give it a push. Suddenly the entire wall of books swings forward. It is a fake bookshelf, hiding a room behind. The Tintin instinct catches me and I wander inside the dark chamber. There are more shelfs of books, perhaps books prohibited to younger ladies. I hear the floor squeaking behind me; someone is approaching. I quickly push back the wall and pretend to look the other way. As a lady walks through the door, I walk out and down the stairs to the bar. Maybe it is better to play Captain Haddock than Tintin for now.

Hidden door / 隱藏的門   Travels book on stack / 書架上的旅遊

Indeed, I have just come from the home of Tintin and Captain Haddock. Brussels is where their creator Herges came from. I visited last week for the first time the three B's - Berlin, Basel and Brussels - despite having been to Europe many times over the years.

My stay in Berlin was necessarily short, so I focused on what was best on offer in this historic capital of Germany. The Berlin Wall, first divisive, then embracive, had already become an icon for all tourists; others could represent me in visiting it. As I stayed within walking distance of Museum Island, which hosted six museums, that's where I spent my day, not least because the ensemble of museums was a UNESCO World Heritage Site. Besides, the stroll along the bank of the river was both pleasant and scenic.

My arrival at Museum Island was a week after the opening of the James Simon Galerie, designed by renowned architect David Chipperfield. As a student of architecture, having written a number of articles for the Architectural Digest since the 1970s, I had already observed the recent architectural trend of museums becoming sculptures in their own right, functions serving style.

The Chipperfield repertoire was a nice exception, finding lines and form that somehow complemented the grand columns of the more classic architecture adjacent to it, while defining old and new with some balance. The underground tunnel to the Neues Museum, built in 1841 and no longer "new," offered connectivity without museum visitors having to go in and out of the building.

The side of Chipperfield's new museum fronting the canal was so minimalist as to become almost like a young lady leaning on an old man – the ancient Pergamon Museum directly next to it. The contrast between the massive

Bode museum / 博物館島

graying columns and the thin white pillars of the Chipperfield was quite stunning.

As an interlude from visiting various Egyptian and classical European exhibits, I had a light lunch in the new café. It offered a great view looking out through the shadow of thin columns into the promenades of the garden below and beyond. Barely opened for a week, the limited menu could be excused. Even the cash register that could not spit up a receipt could be pardoned. But there was a worse crime, bordering on treason, this being Germany. No beer was served! The draft fountain was not working yet.

As I left in the afternoon to walk back to my hotel, the shadow of Chipperfield gradually gave way to another long line of shadow, from the ancient columns of the Neues Museum. At the end of the corridor, an old bearded man, a street musician, was playing a Vivaldi concerto on his violin in the shadows to usher my exit.

My next stop was Basel. I arrived at this historic town in northern Switzerland during the two days which broke heat records throughout Europe. It registered 40° C, highest since records began in the 19th Century.

Basel is famous for Art Basel (the definitive art fair), Basel World (for watches and jewelry) and Auto Basel. But when visiting a city I usually focus on only one main thing, a niche item. Here, it is the Basel Mission.

My quest was triggered some months ago when I passed by Shau Kei Wan, the eastern end of Hong Kong where we use the wet market for our shopping, the closest district to our home in Shek O. At a discreet corner of the old Main Street, I chanced upon a short alley-like road with a slope up the hill. It might have been only twenty meters in length, but the name Basel Road struck my imagination. Further research unveiled its history, with a nearby church and later addition of a school, started by the Basel Mission in 1861. A good friend Marie-Terese living in Basel quickly helped me set up an appointment to visit the Mission during my European tour.

Andrea Rhyn was exceptionally welcoming. The young lady started working as the archivist/historian of the Basel Mission three years ago. After a short introduction and chat in her very heated and somewhat suffocating office, we went down to the basement where the archive was kept behind a vaulted door. Once inside, I did not want to come out, even without knowing what the stacks held; the archive was fully air-conditioned, at 20°C.

James Simon Galerie / 詹姆斯西蒙畫廊　　　Chipperfield's columns / 基帕菲特設計的柱子　　　Lone violinist / 孤獨的小提琴手

The first volume among a long line of rolling shelved cabinets that Andrea Rhyn brought out to show me, however, was warming. They were written and sent from China, albeit from Guangdong where the early missionaries started their work. The handwriting from the 19th Century in many of the reports and diaries was simply awe-inspiring. The penmanship surpassed even printing presses. As much was written in German, including some in an earlier style of script called Suttenlin Handschrift, Andrea Rhyn had to pick segments to translate and entice my interest. These records revealed much regarding life at the time, difficulties with the government, and even personal encounters.

There was even a set of the earliest printed Gospel in Chinese. Next Andrea Rhyn showed me boxes of boxes of material yet to be organized. They had started to digitize early photographs, taken by the missionaries in Hong Kong and Guangdong, but the work was slow and expensive, straining the already tight budget of the Mission. Andrea Rhyn pointed to rows and stacks of wooden boxes on the shelves. I jokingly called these cigar boxes, but inside each box were gelatin-coated glass plates, slides taken during the 19th or early 20th Century. I knew then a treasure trove was here waiting

Belgian waffle choices / 各種的比利時鬆餅

to be deciphered, organized, and interpreted for students of history like myself. For now, Shau Kei Wan and the mystery of Basel Road would have to wait for my return visit.

Next stop, Brussels. My love for mussels may not be well known to friends, but in Brussels, within three days, I had four meals of mussels. The other item good for the palate is waffles. While I am not much into drinking, the Orval beer brewed by Trappist monks, ranked first by many reports and hard to find outside of niche restaurants even in Brussels, was a delight. And Chimay, which is usually among the top three brands in ranks, boasted that it would connect the drinker to God! Karl Marx, who moved from the pubs of London to Brussels, may have found that intoxicating connection while writing his Manifesto in record time.

My old friend David Brooks, who retired three years ago at 54 as Coca-Cola China Chairman, lives here. He had booked me into the Catalonia Hotel, in a posh district of Brussels and away from town center. Its owner was Spanish, thus catered to many Spanish tour groups. Even the gift displays were of Spanish heritage, including of course memorabilia of Gaudi designs. Bacona, a 27 year old Spaniard, was always at the reception desk. She surprised me by always greeting me in Mandarin Chinese. It turned out she could speak Chinese fluently and had

Leading beer Orval & Chimay / 啤酒領導品牌歐瓦樂和奇美   Restaurant at Comic Museum / 漫畫博物館內的餐廳

spent a year and a half at the University of Jilin in northeast China. At the hotel restaurant, an always smiling waitress greeted me in Cantonese. Zhou Xiao Juan was from Huizhou near Hong Kong. She had been here for ten years and had returned home once every year to visit her relatives. There was a direct flight from Brussels to Shenzhen.

A few blocks away was a Chinese-Thai take-out restaurant. Mr Tong, both chef and owner, was from Tiu Keng Leng, that corner of Kowloon east end which used to be swamped with squatter houses for Kuomintang ex-soldiers and refugees. He was now 65 and had arrived 30 years ago. He showed no interest in the current Hong Kong fiasco, as a stable life in Europe was now his anchor.

Hong Kong may have thought itself the center of Asia, but the magnet long ago turned to mainland China, without us Hong Kong people realizing it. Infighting would only accelerate its descent to becoming a second or even third-rate city. Taiwan should take heed, as One Country Three Systems may be around the corner, if two systems is proved not to work. The other option? One Country One System. Push comes to shove, no one should doubt China's resolve in achieving it.

For Brussels, Tintin had come to dominate tourist shops as much as Gaudi defines Barcelona. No visit to Brussels would be complete without a stop at the Comic Museum. I was attracted to the Tintin display in no time, being a long-time fan of that fellow explorer-journalist. My own memorabilia of Tintin had taken up special places at my homes and centers. Before long, I stocked up my collection further, as well as adding other hard-to-find graphic novels. To complement my art background, the one on "Pablo" (Picasso) and another one, entitled "Egon Schiele," seemed must-

read gems.

Finally, I am in London, a city I visited often but am still finding niches to explore. Surely not many frequent visitors to London, nor even Londoners, would know of the University Women's Club. But then, it is not fitting for just anyone, not least a man. Just a block away is David Tang's favorite Dorchester Hotel, where his "Last Rite" farewell dinner party was scheduled too late. I consider hopping over for high tea, but think better of it, considering my limited wardrobe while traveling.

Tour books also do not list Water Rats, a joint where Bob Dylan performed his first gig in 1962. The pub, with separate concert section and a small stage, offers debut or requiem to wannabe artists, especially performing artist types. The house was first built in 1878, and Karl Marx and Lenin were said to have drunk and dined at this establishment, formerly known by the name of Pindar of Wakefield. Marx apparently boarded in a room above the pub.

I make my booking using the trick David Tang taught me, "Table for three. My guest is Kate Moss." His antics worked every time, as he really knew Ms. Moss well. Whereas for me, who never goes to movies or watches TV, I would not even recognize her if she happened to sit at the next table. So, my actual line on the phone is, "This is Dr. Wong. Table for three. I am a journalist writing about London. Near the stage please." Though without David's Queen's English accent, I remember what he would have reminded me, "Always book for one extra person, as you'll be given a bigger table."

I have missed the well-reviewed "f**k Freud" band, which just finished their performance two days ago. But "Dirty

Ol' Crow," performing this weekend, has also received some good reviews. Though the program online said the show began at 7:30 pm, in fact the door to the small theater does not open until 8. After my dinner and a drink outside at the bar, I pay the five Pounds extra for the show.

Several new or near-new singers and bands perform, each group for about half an hour. The "Crows" are supposed to anchor the evening, but by 10 pm, they are still not on stage and I can see the six-man band still drinking outside the pub. One of them is smoking hash. I suppose they need to get higher or stoned before performing their hard rock. That's when I decide to call an Uber to head back to my other, quieter historic club.

The biggest surprise on this London trip happened on Friday. I had a Dim Sum lunch in Chinatown with 90-years-old Sanda Simms, a princess of the Shan State in Myanmar. I had known Sanda for some years and had always been fascinated by her stories. Her father was the first president of independent Burma, but died in prison later under the military regime. Before that tragedy, Sanda and her English husband were adventure seekers, driving a Land Rover from London to Yangon in 1956. She brought me the few pictures she could find from that expedition.

Because of that Land Rover connection, I invited another old friend along. Bill Begg headed Land Rover China, which in time became the biggest market for the auto group, surpassing the US and the UK. Bill had retired at 54, some 13 years ago. Now at 67, he is enjoying traveling, fine food, and playing his violin, and also his Scottish bagpipes.

I knew that Bill's brother James was one of the finest bagpipe makers in the world, creating hand-crafted instruments for leading musicians, champion players, and Army and Police bands. Recently, we took James' son Gavin as our intern in Hong Kong. At the end of lunch when we rose to leave, Bill stopped me and took out from behind him a large bag. Opening it, he showed me a brand-new bagpipe. The gift was for me, made by his brother James. It even had a metal engraving with my name on it.

I left the restaurant carrying with me the large bag containing my "Beggpipe," no doubt a worthy added piece of luggage when I fly back to Hong Kong. Bill has promised to find me a tutor from Hong Kong. The trick will be to also find me a place where I can practice without someone calling the police.

Band performing / 樂團表演

三個 B 開頭的城市

柏林、巴賽爾、布魯塞爾

還有幾個倫敦具歷史秘密的基地

我靜靜地從圖書館緩步而出，走到走廊對面的客廳。對於在這個維多利亞時代圖書館工作的女士們而言，我穿著短袖褲和帆船鞋有點引人注目，或許她們會誤認我是管理員或是俱樂部裡的維修人員。此刻圖書館裡有三位女性，穿著看起來專業又得體。

這個俱樂部創辦於一八八三年，見證一個半世紀以來的歷史，特別是那些受過教育的女性的歷史。這是倫敦的女士大學俱樂部，隱藏在梅菲爾的一個角落。餐廳、圖書館、客廳都是很棒的會場，適合舉辦會議、活動、演講，這裡的講者幾乎都是女性。然而，這裡大多數的設施在本周日都將租借給人辦婚禮。

二十二個房間提供給居住在倫敦外的職業女性會員使用，為了方便她們，可以在這裡待一到兩晚。其中只有三間套房，其他的要共用浴室。這裡的電梯叫「昇降機」，勉強可以擠進三個人，電梯門後還有一個手動的手風琴式金屬捲門。

我很幸運地住進其中一間套房。浴室相當的古老，燈的開關是一條從天花板垂下來的線，開關時都會發出＂滴答＂的聲音。我住進來已經五天了，還沒有見過一位男性，不過也不奇怪，因為這裡只接受女性會員。我則是用香港梅夫人婦女會的會員名義來這裡住宿，香港的婦女會早已經不限只女性會員了。

我對圖書館非常感興趣。這裡讓我想到紐約的耶魯大學俱樂部，我在那裡用餐過好幾次，他們也有個很棒的圖書館。過去幾天我常常安靜地坐在圖書館的舊沙發上看這壁爐，雖然壁爐並沒有生火。這兩年不尋常的熱浪襲擊歐洲和英國，預言未來冷氣機將取代壁爐，進而推進地球暖化。這是多麼地諷刺啊！

當我獨自在圖書館的時候，我總是覺得所有作者的鬼魂都和我在一起。這裡的地板和沙發經常發出聲音，不管是我走路或是坐下來的時候。對於一位老練的作家來說，這裡有一種特有的浪漫和氛圍。瞬間我的眼睛轉向一個裝滿古董書的櫃子，我走過去小心的瀏覽。破損的書擋前有本書寫著「旅遊」。我想要拿這本書但是它卻動也不動。或許太久沒有人讀它，它已經被卡住了。

我注意到矮窗台上有一顆黃銅按鈕。總是好奇的我按了一下。突然間一整面書牆打開了。原來這是個假書櫃，書櫃後面藏著一個密室。丁丁的直覺上身，我走進這黑暗密室。原來這裡還有很多書，可能是不太適合年輕的女士的部份藏書。我聽到地板發出聲音有人從後面走近，於是我趕緊將書牆推回去，假裝沒事。就在一位女士穿過門後，我馬上下樓往吧台走去。也許現在不是當丁丁的時候，應該是要讓阿道克船長出場。

確實我才剛去丁丁和阿道克船長的家。創作者艾爾吉就來自布魯塞爾。儘管我來歐洲這麼多次，上週還是我第一次去了三個都是 B 開頭的城市，柏林、巴賽爾、布魯塞爾。

因為行程關係我在柏林停留的時間很短，所以在這個德國具歷史的首都我只選最經典的地方。柏林圍牆，從前是分裂的象徵，後來敞開雙手，這是所有遊客一定會去參觀的，就由他們代表我去吧。我住的地方只要走一小段路就可以到博物館島，這裡有六家博物館，被聯合國教科文組織指定為世界文化遺產，我在這裡渡過一天。河岸風景幽美，在這散步是很舒服的。

詹姆斯西蒙畫廊才剛開幕一周，出自知名建築師大衛・基帕菲特的設計。身為一個建築學的學生，我從七零年代就給建築文摘《Architectural Digest》寫了好幾篇文章，而我觀察到近來博物館建築物本身儼然已經成為一件雕塑品，功能屈就於風格。

然而基帕菲特的作品是例外，他的線條和型態總是可以融入鄰近經典建築的宏偉立柱裡，在新舊之間找到平衡。地下的通道連接到建於一八四一年的柏林新博物館，其實這個新博物館已經不算「新」了，有了這通道省去遊客需要進進出出博物館的麻煩。

基帕菲特設計的新博物館側面面對著運河，極簡的設計看起來好像一位年輕的女士靠在一位老人身上，那是緊鄰在旁的佩加蒙博物館。佩加蒙博物館巨大的灰色立柱和基帕菲特設計的淺白色柱子之間的對比十分鮮明。

說一個參觀埃及和古典歐洲展覽的插曲，我在新開的咖啡廳吃了個簡單的午餐。這裡看出去的景觀很美，立柱的影子延伸到下面花園長廊的遠處。因為才剛開幕不到一周，我可以體諒餐點沒有什麼選擇，也可以體諒收銀機吐不出收據，但是最不可想像的事，幾乎是刑事級的犯罪，這裡是德國，居然沒有啤酒，生啤酒機仍然未能運作！

下午時分我離開這裡往飯店走，基帕菲特的影子逐漸變成古老的柏林新博物館柱子。走廊盡頭有一位滿臉鬍子的老人，一位街頭音樂家，他在列柱的陰影下用小提琴演奏維瓦第協奏曲，音樂一路陪伴著我。

下一站，巴賽爾。我抵達這個瑞士北邊的古城時，那兩天熱浪破了歐洲的紀錄。四十度，超出了自十九世紀以來所有的紀錄。

巴賽爾知名，是因為巴賽爾藝術博覽會（最具權威的藝術博覽會），巴賽爾世界（手錶和珠寶）還有巴賽爾車展。但是通常我去一個城市都只會專注在一件事情上，這次，是巴賽爾的崇真會。

幾個月前經過筲箕灣的時候激起我對崇真會的好奇，筲箕灣在港島的東端，是離我們石澳的家最近的地區，我們會在這裡的菜市場採購日用所需。當時我路過一個斜坡小巷，就在一個不起眼的老街角落裡，這條名為巴賽爾的小路大概只有二十公尺長，卻引發了我的好奇心。於是我進一步去研究它的歷史，原來連同附近的一座教堂，以及後來增設的學校都是由在一八六一年創辦的崇真會所建立的。一位住在巴賽爾的好朋友瑪麗·特瑞莎很快地幫我預約，安排我去歐洲時參觀這所教會。

安德亞·萊恩很熱情。這位年輕的女士三年前以檔案／歷史學家在崇真會工作。在她悶熱的辦公室裡簡短地寒暄後，我們走到地下室，檔案存放在拱形門後。一進去之後我就不想出來了，即使不知道裡面有什麼東西，最重要的是，這裡的涼度控制在二十度。

Archive slides in "cigar boxes" / 檔案室的幻燈片放在「雪茄盒」裡　　　　English & Chinese scripts / 英文和中文的手稿

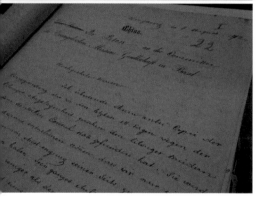

Early Gospel in Chinese / 早期的中文福音
Early missionary manuscripts / 早期傳教士的手稿

從一長排的滾輪書櫃中，安德亞拿出的第一個檔案就讓我備感溫暖。這些都是在中國書寫後寄出的，從廣東，崇真會開始活動的地方。這些十九世紀的手寫的報告、日記真是令人驚嘆。書寫的字跡更是勝過印刷。大多是德文，一些是用更古老的 *Suttenlin Handschrift* 字體，安德亞還特地挑出來翻譯給我聽，非常吸引我。這些紀錄透露當時的生活，他們遇到與政府交涉的困難，還有個人的遭遇。

這裡還有一套最早印刷的中文福音書。接著安德亞給我看一盒盒還沒有被整理的素材。他們開始將傳教士在香港和廣東拍的舊照片數位化，過程很慢也很昂貴，因為崇真會的預算吃緊。安德亞指向櫃子上一整疊的箱子，我開玩笑地說那些雪茄盒，但是裡面都是十九世紀和二十世紀初上了明膠塗層的玻璃板、幻燈片。我知道裡面有許多在歷史上具有意義的寶貝等著被解碼、整理、詮釋。現在，關於筲箕灣和巴賽爾道的事要等我將來回來再說。

下一站，布魯塞爾。許多朋友可能不知道我很喜歡青口，在布魯塞爾的三天裡我就吃了四次青口。另外一個好吃的東西是鬆餅。我本身是沒有那麼愛喝酒，但是修道院釀造的歐瓦樂啤酒評比很高，即使在布魯塞爾也只有特定的餐廳才有得賣，真是支好喝的啤酒。還有奇美啤酒，排名前三的品牌，他們很自豪於自己的啤酒可以讓人們與上帝搭上線。卡爾・馬克思從倫敦的酒吧喝到布魯塞爾的酒吧，也許他在那醉人的時刻，以創紀錄的時間寫下他的共產主義宣言。

我的一位老友大衛·布魯克住在這裡，他在五十四歲的時候從中國可口可樂總裁的位子退休。他幫我訂了一家加泰羅尼亞飯店，在一個高級的區域，遠離市中心。飯店老闆是西班牙人，接待不少西班牙的觀光團。連禮品也帶著西班牙傳統風，裡面當然還有高第的紀念品。巴蔻娜，二十七歲的西班牙人總是在櫃檯。她總是用中文問候我，讓我感到很驚訝。她在東北的吉林大學待了一年半，說的一口流利的國語。飯店的餐廳裡有位女服務生總是微笑地用廣東話問候我。趙曉娟來自鄰近香港的惠州，她來這裡已經十年了，每年都會回老家去看親友。從布魯塞爾有直飛的班機到深圳。

幾個街區外有個中國菜和泰國菜的外帶餐廳。唐先生是這裡的廚師也是老闆，來自九龍東角的調景嶺，那裡以前有好多國民黨退下來的軍人和難民居住的違章建築。唐先生現在已經六十五歲了，他在三十年前來到這裡。唐先生對香港面前的混亂狀況一點興趣也沒有，因為他現在在歐洲有個安定的家。

香港可能認為自己是亞洲的中心，但是這中心不久前已經慢慢往中國靠近了，但是我們香港人並不了解。內鬥只會讓它成為二流甚至是三流的城市。台灣應該注意，倘若兩制是失敗的，那麼一國三制或許已經逼近。其他的選項是什麼？一國一制。推擠造成衝撞，沒有人會懷疑中國的能力與決心。

就像高第在巴塞隆納一樣，丁丁佔據了布魯塞爾的每一家觀光禮品店。到布魯塞爾沒去比利時漫畫藝術中心就好像沒來過一樣。我馬上被丁丁的展覽吸引，我一直是他的粉絲，跟我一樣他不只是探險家，也是記者。我收藏的丁丁紀念品在我家和中心佔據了重要的位置。不用多久我就買了些收藏品，還有一本很難買到的圖像小說。因為對藝術的喜好，我也買了一本《巴勃羅》（畢加索），還

Comic Museum / 漫畫博物館
Display at museum / 博物館裡的展覽
Colorful comic / 多彩的漫畫

有另一本《埃貢‧席勒》，看起來好像也是一本我應必讀的書。

最後我到倫敦，一個我經常拜訪的城市，雖說如此，但總是可以找到值得探險的地方。肯定許多常來的觀光客甚至是倫敦人都不知道倫敦的女子大學俱樂部。不過，這也不是一個所有人都可以來的地方，特別是男士。一個街區外就是鄧永鏘爵士最喜歡的多徹斯特酒店，他生前希望在生命離開之前可以跟親朋好友們在這裡再聚一次，但是餐會的時間訂的太晚了。我本來想去喝個下午茶，但是想想我出門旅行時的穿著還是算了。

觀光旅遊書不會介紹 Water Rats 這個巴布‧狄倫曾經在一九六二年首演過的地方。這家酒館有個獨立的演唱區還有個小舞台給那些想要成為音樂人初次登台表演的機會。這棟房子是一八七八年建的，以前叫 Pindar of Wakefield，聽說卡爾‧馬克思和列寧都曾經在這裡吃過飯喝過酒。馬克思甚至還曾經住過這酒館的樓上。

我訂位時都會用鄧永鏘爵士教我的一招，「我要訂位，三人。我的客人是凱特‧摩絲」。他這招很管用，但是他真的認識凱特‧

Water Rats Pub / Water Rats 酒吧
The "Crows" outside Pub / 「The Crows」樂團在酒吧外

摩絲本人。而我，又不看電影或電視，即使她坐在我旁邊我也不會知道她是誰。所以我訂位時是這樣說「我是黃博士，我要訂三人的位子。我是記者，來倫敦採訪。請給我靠近舞台的位子。」雖然沒有鄧永鏘爵士的英女皇口音，但是我記得他這麼提醒過我「一定要多訂一個人的位子，這樣他們才會給你大一點的桌子」。

評論很好的「f**Freud」樂團兩天前才在這裡表演，很可惜我錯過了。這個周末表演的「Dirty Ol' Crow」評價不錯。雖然網路上說表演晚上七點半開始，但其實表演廳要到八點才開門。在酒吧外吃了晚飯也喝了一杯後，我付了五英鎊去看秀。

好幾個新的樂團或是還算是有點新的樂團各表演三十分鐘。「Dirty Ol' Crow」應該是今晚的主秀，但是到了十點，他們還沒有上台，六位團員還在外面喝酒，其中一位在抽大麻。我猜他們需要有點飄飄然才有辦法上台表演重搖滾吧。這時候我決定叫一台 Uber 回去我的另一個俱樂部，一個安靜許多，並且有歷史的地方。

這趟去倫敦最大的驚喜是那個周五。我和九十歲的 Sanda Simms 緬甸撣邦的公主在中國城裡吃港式點心。我認識 Sanda 好多年了，她的故事非常吸引我。她的父親是緬甸獨立後第一位總統，但是後來死在軍政府的監獄裡。在這災難發生之前，Sanda 和她的英籍丈夫都愛探險，曾在一九五六年從倫敦開荒原路華一路到仰光。她還帶了一些照片給我看。

因為和荒原路華的關係，我邀請了另一位老朋友一起吃飯。Bill Begg 曾負責路華在中國的市場，現在這個市場已經超過英國和美國，是路華全球最大的市場了。十三年前，Bill 在他五十四歲的時候退休。現在他六十七歲，生活很愜意，享受旅遊、美食、拉小提琴還有玩他的蘇格蘭風笛。

我知道 Bill 的兄弟 James 是世界上最頂尖的風笛製作達人，手做樂器給世界級的樂手，還有軍警樂隊。不久前 James 的兒子 Gavin 到香港來當我們的實習生。吃完午餐後我們起身要離席時，Bill 叫住我然後從背後拿出一個大袋子，一打開，裡面是一個全新的風笛。那是送給我的禮物，James 親手做的，上面還刻了我的名字。

離開餐廳時帶了一個屬於我的風笛，回香港的行李又多了一件。Bill 答應我會在香港幫我找一個風笛家教。但是重點是我要找一個可以練習的地方，才不會有被騷擾的鄰居打電話給警察。

Bill Begg with HM / Bill Begg 和 HM

國
王
與
我

THE KING AND I

Thimphu, Bhutan – August 20, 2019

THE KING AND I

"I would occasionally initiate a meeting if I heard that someone interesting was visiting our country, but I am quite selective about it," said the King as we walked up the steps of the Amankora. I assume the person he is interested in is my friend Vic Lee, whose family is traveling with me to Bhutan. After all, he is known as a co-founder of Tencent, in charge of its operations and the building of the internet giant's technology platform.

But His Majesty's gestures of welcome were extended to us well before we even met. First, he opened his "summer" palace adjacent to the grand Punakha Dzong, a castle-like edifice housing both the government and monastic body. A sumptuous lunch was prepared on our behalf, with guards and servants in attendance. The final menu was even revised by order of Her Majesty the Royal Grandmother.

Her Majesty has treated me as if she is my patron saint during my most recent visits to Bhutan. Having two palace flag cars with her favorite security guard in full attendance since arriving at the airport now seems routine. She not only offered lunch and tea for me at her Palace, but also opened her historic Bhutan House in Kalimpong during my visit last year. Occasionally she sends gifts,

Punakha Dzong / 普納卡宗寺廟

including carrying by hand a gold-gilt statue to Hong Kong, as well as books, private manuscripts and letters sent by mail.

Her granddaughter, Princess or Ashi "Baby" Kesang, and Ugyen, a close confidante of the King, made up the rest of our entourage as we traveled in and out of the capital Thimphu. Perhaps it was due to Her Majesty's kind reference that we are being received by her grandson the Fifth King of Bhutan.

At a faraway medicinal hot spring in Gasa Dzong to the north, our group stopped to visit the many open-air pools, each listing a different temperature and for treatment of varying ailments. The locals from far and wide come

A palace-prepared traveling buffet / 皇宮準備給我們旅行時吃的餐點
How Man in King's bath / HM 使用國王的溫泉

to soak in this famous hot spring. A road making it more accessible was completed only four years ago - even the royal entourage used to come on horseback, taking days.

Above the civilian pools is a walled "Rest House." This is the Royal Hot Spring Retreat of the King. Two uniformed guards opened the door with a walkway toward the rather modest abode. Inside is a wooden bath around ten-foot square, with steaming spring water piped in from the outside. There are two sofas set on the side of the pool, with a small bathroom next to it for changing. A bedroom is situated adjacent to the pool. On the wall is a picture of the Fourth King, with the current Fifth King and his Queen. On an opposite wall is a picture of the young crown prince, now three and a half years old.

Somehow, I felt I was trespassing. I took a few pictures and was ready to leave, feeling privileged to get a glimpse of His Majesty's private pool, which even Ashi, the princess, had never entered, let alone used. She had just visited the hot spring outside some four months ago. "But the King has ordered that the pool should be open for your use," quipped Ashi in her

Entrance to King's summer retreat palace at Punakha /
進入國王在普納卡宗寺夏宮的入口

usual quiet and soft whispering voice. Now, that was a most beautiful song to my ears. "I will come back after dinner," I tried to sound cool among the hot air and answered, as if it was no big deal. The steam was rising from the bath and beginning to wet my eyes. I must make sure no one thinks I am moved to tears!

Fast forward to my meeting with the King the following evening. I suppose it was hastily organized. We received word of the meeting at the very last minute when some of us were in the shower, others scattered around after the long trip to Gasa and participated in a once-a-year religious festival. We had to scramble and arrived at the gate of the Aman, standing on ceremony. Not long after, His Majesty arrived in a van just as it was turning dark in the evening. Tall and thin, he came out of the car and we walked together to an antechamber for our meeting. Because of the venue, our meeting that ensued was rather candid, revealing even some less known and private matters of the King.

Festival babies / 參加慶典的嬰兒

He certainly made an effort for us to feel relaxed, mentioning more than once that he is a humble man in front of his people. Nothing seemed orchestrated and he chatted with impromptu openness, telling us of his vision for his country. "We cannot forget our past, but we must look into the future." Indeed, he talked about the future for the first half hour, defining his vision for a land-locked nation sandwiched not only between the high Himalayas to the north and the jungle to the south, but also between two formidable countries, India and China. The delicate balance he has to toe was obvious beyond his words. A half an hour into our meeting, he apologized, "This is getting to be like a monologue." From then on, I chimed in as much as I could, mustering the little that I knew of Bhutan.

"Tourism is good, it enriched our country's economy. But it also comes with a footprint, including some of the less desirable things people bring along," he noted. Our discussion turned to nano satellites, when his voice became more excited, with hand gestures to illustrate his point. "These miniature satellites, just like tiny boxes, would be delivered into space orbit in large numbers, and Bhutan, with all its huge supply of hydro-electric power, is in a perfect position to provide the laser receiver needed for satellite to satellite communications," said the King. His grasp of modern science and technology is certainly ahead of me, and I started to lose the trail of his

Gasa religious festival / 迦薩宗教盛會

explanation, despite having used so much satellite data from the 1970s all the way into application of data collected by the second Space Shuttle in 1981. With almost the same breath, he talked about the panoptes telescope, the latest and less expensive astronomical devices to be deployed in a remote locations.

He quizzed Vic regarding how to build a high-tech platform in Bhutan, such that what may be difficult to implement at a large scale in other countries might first be experimented here in a small country with fewer people, and if successful then scaled up and applied to the rest of the world. Vic concurred and explained that neither he himself nor founder Pony Ma of Tencent came from elite universities, as Shenzhen doesn't rank high enough to be among the top 100, or even 200, in the world. Nonetheless, it did not prevent them from entering the market with a new and disruptive idea and application in the internet world.

"We love WeChat. Our entire country is using WeChat, especially in all the remote areas. Where people cannot write or type, they can use their voice to communicate," said the King. By then, we were almost an hour into our conversation and felt far more relaxed. I was tempted at this point to ask for his WeChat QR code, but thought better of it.

"You know how I got to know so much about IT and people surrounding technology?" asked the King. "It was all because of Meng." He did not reference who this Meng was, except that he was from Singapore and an executive from Google. I guessed it had to be Chade-Meng Tan. I was not sure if the King knew the latest development about Meng, who had left the outfit he founded under

some uncomfortable circumstances. I kept my mouth shut and just listened.

"The Queen was heavily pregnant and I went to Singapore with her. I wanted to be very low-key, thus rented an apartment to stay rather than in a hotel," the King recounted. "At night, someone came knocking on my door. I opened and here this guy introduced himself as Meng, saying he's in my neighboring apartment and he apologized," he continued. "Apologize for what? I did not hear any noise, so I said. Obviously he did not know who I am anyway," said the King. "Then he apologized profusely again, that the smell of the durian was from his apartment. I said, Great, I love durian, bring it over and we will enjoy it together," the King ended his story with a laugh. Thus Meng and the King became fast friends, and Meng introduced him to many IT experts later on.

"You know I took on the role as King when I was 26 before formal coronation at 28, and now I am 39," said the King as his topic made a turn. "Recently, I presided over the university graduation commencement. I told four thousand young graduates that when I ascended the throne, they would have been in first grade, and now they

Ashi, Vic & wife Chris / Ashi，Vic 和夫人 Chris

Bhutanese at festival / 參加盛會的不丹人

國王與我

「我偶爾會主動邀請有意思的外賓見面，但是我會仔細挑選。」當我們一起走上阿曼喀拉階梯時，國王這樣跟我說。我想國王指的是我的朋友 *Vic Lee*，這趟他的家人跟我們一起來不丹。*Vic Lee* 是騰訊的共同創辦人，負責營運和平台建構。

國王陛下為了表示歡迎我們，在接見之前就已經指示官員要好好招待我們。首先他開放在普納卡宗寺廟旁的夏宮讓我們參觀，那個城堡一般的宗教建築是政府機構也是寺廟。當然，午餐也是極為豐盛，菜單還是由皇太后母陛下修改確認過的。午餐時警衛和服務人員也全程陪伴。

皇太后母陛下就好像是我在不丹的守護神，每次都會派兩輛插著皇宮旗子的車和她最喜歡的保全人員來機場接我。她不僅僅邀請我到皇宮吃午飯、喝茶，去年她還開放了一間歷史悠久，位於卡寧朋的不丹宅院供我參觀和午餐。偶爾她也會寄禮物給我，還有一次特地托人手提一個鍍金雕像到香港，她有時候也會寄書、私人手稿也會寫信給我。

她的孫女，*Ashi Kesang* 公主，還有國王的知己 *Ugyen* 陪伴我們一行人穿梭在首都廷布。也許是因為皇太后母陛下的美言，她的孫子，第五任不丹國王接見了我們。

Gate to King's bath / 通往國王溫泉的大門　　　　　Door to King's bath / 通往國王溫泉的內門

我們去了個具有療效的溫泉區，在加薩宗北方，距離市區有點遙遠。那裏有好幾個戶外溫泉，每個都有不同的溫度和療效，不只當地人，連外地遊客都會來這裡。四年前進入這裡的路才鋪好，以前皇室成員可是要騎上好幾天的馬才能到達這裡。

這裡有個專屬於國王的皇室溫泉會所，位於一般百姓使用的溫泉上方，是個有圍牆的「休憩屋」。兩位穿著制服的警衛為我們開了門，門後步道一路延伸到一棟相當低調的建築物。裡面有一個大約十英尺平方大的木製溫泉池，冒著煙的溫泉水從外面引進。溫泉旁有兩組沙發，旁邊還有個小間的更衣室。溫泉旁的房間牆上掛有一張第四任，以及現在第五任的國王和皇后的相片。對面的牆上掛的則是皇太子的，現年三歲半。

能夠進去一探國王的私人溫泉，讓我覺得好像闖入私人禁地，卻也感到備受禮遇。Ashi 公主連進都沒進來過，更不用說在這裡泡溫泉了。我拍了幾張照片後準備離開。公主用她一貫的輕聲細語對我說：「國王下令說這個溫泉開放給你使用。」這話聽來真是悅耳。事實上，公主四個月前曾經來過

Ashi "baby" Kesang / Ashi 公主

這個溫泉區，但只能用到外面的溫泉。「我晚餐後再來吧」熱氣渺渺的空間裡，我用很酷的方式回答她，好像這不是件大事。蒸氣充滿整個溫泉也弄濕了我的眼睛，我得確定沒有人以為我是感動到掉淚才行！

快轉到隔天晚上我和國王的會面，這個會面的邀約來的很倉促。就在參加迦薩一年一度的宗教盛會後，我們有些人還在洗澡，有些人正在休息，國王要接見我們的訊息突然送到。於是我們趕緊衝到阿曼門口等待。那時天剛暗下，不多久，國王坐著廂型車前來，他看起來又高又瘦，下車後我們一起走進接待室。因為會面的場所，讓我們的對話相當坦率，國王也告訴我一些比較不為外人所知的事。

國王非常很用心地要讓我們放鬆，不只一次說在人民面前他是個謙卑的人。他很自然地跟我們聊天，告訴我們這個國家未來的藍圖。「我們不能忘記我們的過去，但是我們也必需往前看。」的確，關於未來的遠景他講了半個鐘頭。這內陸國家北部被喜馬拉雅山脈夾住，南部處於叢林之間，四週還被大國印度和中國包圍。他事事都得拿捏得當，顧慮周全。談了半小時後，他賠不是的說：「怎麼好像變成了我個人的獨白了！」接下來我也加入談話，並試著談一些我了解的不丹事情。

Punakha adjacent coronation hall / 普納卡宗寺廟旁的加冕禮堂

口，就連絕育都沒辦法解決這個問題。」

「你知道不只藏獒犬很特別，連他們的『瑪曲藏馬』也是很優秀的。為了在普那卡宗舉行我的加冕儀式，我特別用卡車載了十匹這種馬到邊境，翻山越嶺，就是為了讓牠們和一頭大象一起加入遊行的隊伍。」國王跟我們分享他在十幾年前就很喜歡的這種馬。「這樣，我應該找幾匹這種馬載些藏獒犬過來，剛好一石二鳥！」我打趣的說。

「皇太子他現在三歲半。照顧他的都是本地人，跟他說不丹語，所以他的本國語說的很好。除此之外他也開始學習中文。」國王說。與我們分享這樣關於私人的事或許會讓我們覺得更親密，加上我們又都是從香港來的。瞬間，我想到香港街頭上的紛亂，我從沒見過或想像過這些事會發生在這個跟我有七十年關係的城市。我想起已過世的第三任不丹國王曾說過：「當他們要求民主的時候千萬不要給他們，最好是在他們要求前就給他們。」他的見解真是有道理，第四任國王聽進去了，也執行了，而且享譽全球。

我們談了兩個鐘頭，大多是國王有興趣的話題，涵蓋的層面很廣，有時也很深入。然後，隨扈送上國王準備送給我們的禮物。他給我們每人一把普巴，類似匕首那樣的宗教文物，用來保護我們的幸福。Vic 的兒子 Alex 收到這個禮物後非常高興。在阿曼的古董商店裡他看上一件類似的東西，標價美金一千零七十二元；而這把國王送的普巴則是無價的。

當我們跟著國王起身準備離開時，國王突然停了下來並彎下腰給 Vic 九歲的兒子一個大大的擁抱。然後他注意到李伯達用了一個外型特別的小相機在拍我們，那個相機有個圓形的閃光燈。國王於是要求看一下那台相機，說：「我也很喜歡拍照，現在甚至還會用底片相機拍照。我最新的那台萊卡很棒但實在是太貴了。」我不想炫耀我曾經跟萊卡老闆安德裏亞斯·考夫曼吃過兩次飯，並且還受邀到位於德國韋茨拉爾的萊卡的新總部，甚至還是在開幕的前一天去參觀。

國王欣賞這兩台相機，一台是用來微距攝影或是浮潛時用，另一台小的則是用在即時影像。他也提到舊型的哈蘇相機背後還有拍立得。我說等我們把照片都下載後會把這兩台新相機馬上送過來當作回禮。我還會一併寄上印有我拍的照片在上面的氂牛圍巾。國王提醒我要在上面簽名，因為他會把它裱框展示。

我的皇室探訪之旅還沒結束。接下來的幾天我和皇太后陛下見了兩次面，兩次都在她的皇宮。我們認識多年已經是彼此信賴的朋友。離開前，和她見第二次面時，我帶著我的好友 Gilbert 和 Queenie Wong 一起。皇太后陛下對待他們就像她的老友一樣。後來陛下告訴我，Gilbert 很像她過世的哥哥，不丹的前總理，這勾起許多她的回憶。

離別時皇太后陛下贈送他們一個鍍金的雕像。她送我的則是她兩天前挑的另一個鍍金湯東傑布雕像，成為我的守護者。這位智者

Her Majesty, How Man & rainbow /
皇太后陛下和 HM 還有彩虹

Thangtonng Gyalpo statue / 湯東傑布雕像

生活在七百多年前，被視為多個領域頂尖的專家，從科學到工程到藝術。據稱他在西藏和不丹建造了五十八座鐵索橋，有些到現在還存在。為了募集資金造橋，他創造了西藏戲劇，由七位美麗的姊妹組成的團體到處去表演。他也是傑出的建築師，興建西藏和不丹一些最著名的寺廟。*CERS* 和 *Gilbert* 也參與贊助其中一個寺廟的修復工程。

我收到的這尊雕像可不是一般的湯東傑布雕像。皇太后陛下挑了二十幾個才覺得這個最適合送給我。我覺得我好像應該幫這位顯赫的神製作一部紀錄片才對，只可惜出了喜馬拉雅山之外，知道祂的人並不多。

當我離開陛下皇宮時剛好有個彩虹落在遠方的山丘上。不久後變成了雙道彩虹。陛下和她九十六歲的姊姊 *Ashi Tashi* 跟我說這是個吉兆。她還說，我跟第五任國王見面的那天，在加薩區一年一度的祭典見到的那位第七十任大方丈是位轉世的喇嘛，一位仁波切，是這國度位階最高的僧人。就這樣，一天之內我見了兩位地位崇高的人，一位是地上的，一位是天上的。嗡嘛呢叭咪吽，願因果與我同在！

Her Majesty with Gilbert & Queenie / 皇太后陛下和 Gilbert 還有 Queenie

孟巴族

MONPAS

Trongsa, Bhutan – Aug. 15, 2019

MONPAS
An ethnic group with fewer than 400 remaining

"I was tempted to say a television would be good, but somehow I held back," said Lhajay the village chief. We chatted a bit more casually over tea before I took leave from his village. My question was about what the village might need that we could help with. I suggested a television as I could see that there was no TV antenna in sight within the entire village, or in any home, whereas they do have electricity. A full screen TV would have cost us less than USD500.

Instead Lhajay hesitated before answering, somewhat timidly, "Wangling, the next Monpa village, has both a husking machine and a milling machine to make flour. It would be wonderful if our village could have the same. It would save the villagers a lot of time and labor, thus allowing us to do more of other chores." It must seem like a tall order to ask for such items. After all, the two machines together would cost USD4500, an unthinkable sum for Jingbi, a village of less than 200 people who all require government assistance to subsist during any year with a bad harvest.

Through Ugyen, my traveling companion who was translating for me, I offered that CERS would donate the two machines. As always, I elaborated, "This is not my money, but from friends who trust my judgement." We then sat down for some mint tea and a few pieces of "melon." When I say melon, it is an overstatement. The best fruit they could muster for guests were cucumber slices. That was what they served us earlier at the best home in the village, and now again. Soon we'll be on the road heading back to Trongsa, the small regional community under which Jingbi village is administered. Trongsa, situated in the south of the country, is still six hours by car from Thimphu, the capital of Bhutan. And the Trongsa Dzong is a huge castle-like edifice which houses both the monastic body as well as the region's government offices.

Despite the difficult terrain of jungle and hillocks here inside the Black Mountain National Park, mobile service has reached this distant village of Jingbi. I Googled "Monpa Bhutan" and a few short items showed up. The people here are not to be confused with the larger Monpa ethnic groups of different origins in southern Tibet and in Arunachal Pradesh of eastern India. The special population of Monpa here in Bhutan is variously reported to be less than 400 and 600 individuals maximum.

CERS has always focused on niches, neglected or undervalued cultural and natural phenomena, be it people, animals or hidden ecosystems. We are not unlike investors looking for undervalued companies to buy. In this case, we are not only focused on a largely hidden community, but also a relatively hidden country. Big data and its analysis have little to do with our kind of work, as impact in such cases of vulnerable people is measured by multiples of the norm.

Bhutan is known for its Gross National Happiness (GNH) index, pristine environment, well-preserved religious sites, and high-end resorts, on the bucket list of "discerning" tourists. Little known are the Monpa, a people now left with perhaps less than 400 individuals, an estimate based on local anthropologist Seeta Giri's research almost twenty years ago. Yet by many accounts, the Monpa were the original inhabitants of this Himalayan country, today formally known as the Kingdom of Bhutan, as it was ruled by a traditional king.

Our visit is to update of Seeta's work, though our current study is more basic and not as systematic. First of all is the riddle of the discrepancy in population count; 400 to 600 - that's a 50% variance. But if one looks at other demographic figures of Bhutan, comparing past to present, perhaps the riddle can be solved.

A cover article in the National Geographic published in 1974, during the coronation of the 4th king, cited a population of 1.1 million for the kingdom. Today, the official figure is barely 700,000. Some of the decline is because of a forced and voluntary exodus of well over 100,000 Nepali-speaking Lhotshampa people in the 1990's. Bhutan apparently feared the precedent of neighboring Sikkim gradually being overrun by outside ethnic groups to ultimately becoming an Indian State in 1975.

But that high 1974 figure is also now generally acknowledged as having been inflated to allow Bhutan to receive more aid from the World Bank, UNICEF, or other international outfits by drawing the average household income and per capita GDP downward, thus classifying Bhutan as a poorer nation. Listing the Monpa with a population of 600 may well have been an extension of that exaggeration. Today, methods of survey and cross-checking produce far more accurate and less shady results.

At the home of Nidup, arguably the best home in the village, we conducted some interviews. Several villagers, both men and women, crowded into the sitting/dining cum shrine room to greet us. Though only 53 years old, his graying curly hair, probably coupled with a hard life, makes him seem much older. Nidup is the local rice wine brewer as well as head carpenter. Whenever a new house is to be built, he would be called upon.

Before any questions could be asked, there was a short ceremony whereby the group would sing a welcoming song while serving the guests three rounds of wine. From then on, the villagers joined in the merry drinking. That ceremony, however, was preceded by sprinkling a bit of wine to honor the Buddhist deity sitting upon the shrine. Despite observing Buddhism, the village also has one male shaman whose service is called upon when needed. A bowl of "fruits" was offered in front of us. It consisted of a few eggs, corn, banana, pomegranate, sugarcane and a cucumber. That, apparently, is the best they could present to guests.

Nidup's household has seven persons. His mother maintains her own house, as Monpa families are matriarchal. Only the eldest daughter stayed

Offering wine and fruits / 供奉酒和水果
Nidup's daughter / Nidup 的女兒
HM's hemp hat & nettle cape / HM 的大麻帽和蕁麻披肩

with the mother and would inherit the house from her. Nidup thus established his own household with his wife, four children and a maternal uncle. His eldest is a son, now serving as a monk in Sikkim. His daughter, now 23, second among the siblings, has just gotten married to a driver and the two of them are expected to live with her parents, and ultimately inherit their property. The other children, one boy and one girl, are expected to establish their own homes once they are married.

Nidup has six acres of land, growing two crops each year, rotating between rice in the summer and wheat in the winter. They also grow some corn and sugarcane. He will receive only half the harvest, as his land is farmed by a tenant farmer who takes the other half. On their land, they also grow fruit, like bananas, papayas, mangoes and pomegranate. As to livestock, the family owns ten cattle; two of them are dairy cows, producing milk only when they have calves. The cattle are not slaughtered since the family is Buddhist.

Soon our topic turned to the village. At that point, the other villagers joined in the chat and helped answer any questions I raised. There are 22 families within Jingbi with a population of 172. The village school has 55 students, six of whom are children of the teachers who are sent in from outside by the government. There are also six students from a neighboring village, and they board at the school in an adjacent building. It is a primary school, from first to sixth grade. The school was built in 1995 with support of the Fourth King's uncle. Water supply reached the village for the first time in 1992. Being Buddhists, young men may join the temple. Here in Jingbi, twelve men have become monks, and there are three nuns, living away in a nunnery.

The traditional bamboo houses are all gone. Today the Monpa live in wooden houses with stone walls and metal roofs, not too different from the mainstream Bhutanese, though less decorative and more spartan. The building of these houses was supported by the royal family. There are almost no visitors from the outside as the three villages inhabited by the Monpa, Jingbi, Wangling and Phumzur people are all out of the way. Only Jingbi is accessible by road, since 2011, and a hike to Wangling would take two hours for the locals, and possibly double that for us. There are two rituals annually, one in March or April, the other on December 10 each year, when the village has a festival and all the villagers gather for two days of ritual, drinking and dancing.

Traditionally, the Monpa were hunter/gatherers and knew much about ethnobotany, including what could be consumed and used as medicine. But much of that knowledge is eclipsing as lifestyles have begun to change. The weaving of fabric using nettle and hemp stalk fiber is also disappearing. Only two women who knew how to do it remain. I could see that Nidup's daughter could use a hand loom to weave, but she wove modern dyed yarn. At another home, I came across a lady who still can collect, spin and weave with nettle. We secured a specimen of a piece of nettle cape used to protect the back while carrying loads in the forest. Hemp is grown everywhere. While hiking, the Monpa picked some fresh hemp and fashioned a crowned hat for me to shade myself from the scorching sun. Unfortunately, a hat made from marijuana would not go through customs well if I were to bring it home.

The Monpa used to go hunting, using bows with poison arrows. Going into the forest in groups of two to three, chasing after boars, bear, deer and porcupine which frequent nearby hills. Occasionally they still see tiger footprint but have never gotten any. If their hunt is successful, every villager would receive some game meat. There are hornbills as well. Villagers know that the male locks up the female in a tree hole to lay her eggs, after which he would fetch food to feed the mother and hatchlings. Villagers never harm the hornbill.

Bhurba is 32 years of age. He is one of the very few Monpa who still hunt. He offered to take us to his house ten minutes away to observe how a ground arrow is set up as a trap. Ten minutes turned out to be over thirty minutes, much of it uphill. "Just a little ahead," came the answer every time I asked how much further. Distance and time calculations were quite synonymous with other hill tribes I had traveled with, be they continents apart.

Over the ridge, we walked through bamboo groves, pine forests, and more hemp bushes. A lone house, isolated from all the other village houses and hidden among the bushes, was Bhurba's home. I arrived at the tail of our small entourage and saw Bhurba already setting up his trap in the backyard. It resembled more a ground crossbow with a wooden piece as center axis. The arch of the bow was very long, perhaps over six feet in length. When fully stretched, the bow string must have carried over fifty kilos.

Bhurba demonstrated how the ground crossbow is set, with a string across the animal's path that triggers the firing. He said once the trap is set, he would go check on it regularly, and perhaps once in a month they might get an animal. Both collecting and hunting is gradually becoming obsolete, as young people do not want to learn such hardy tasks anymore. For big game, the arrows are charged with a very potent poison extracted from the root of a plant. Such a toxin might also have special medical or research applications and should be studied.

As we began our trip back from Jingbi Village, while the car made the switch-backs down the hill, our driver suddenly stopped and pointed into the forest. There near us was a large group of

monkeys jumping from tree top to tree top. As I got out of the car, Ugyen told me that these were the famous Golden Langur.

I suddenly remembered the book Mammals of Bhutan that Ugyen had given me a couple days before. Turning to page 9 of the book, the Golden Langur was there with a nice drawing and a map. The first two lines described it, "Its golden coloration and behavior endears it to the Bhutanese. The langur does not raid crops and is considered a good omen when sighted on a journey."

Indeed, I did consider it a good omen to see these rare primates as we ended our first visit to the Monpa.

孟巴族

只剩下不到四百人的原住民族

「本來是想要一台電視機的，但我還是忍住沒說。」村長 *Lhajay* 告訴我。離開這個村子前我們邊喝茶邊聊了一下。我問他村子有什麼需要，或許我們可以幫得上忙。我問他說要不要一台電視，因為整個村子裡我看不到一個電視天線，但他們是有電力的。一台大尺寸平面電視用不到美金五百元。

Lhajay 猶豫了一下，有點不好意思地說：「孟巴村隔壁的 *Wangling* 村有脫殼機和磨粉機可以製作麵粉。我們村子如果也有的話那就太好了。可以省下村民很多時間跟體力，讓我們去做更多別的事。」這個要求有點高，畢竟兩台機器加起來要美金四千五百元，對 *Jingbi* 村來說是個難以想像的數字。這村子人口還不到兩百人，農作物歉收的時候甚至還需要政府的補助才能生存。

透過 *Ugyen*，我們隨行的朋友進行翻譯溝通，我提議探險學會捐贈這兩台機器。一如我經常說的，「這些不是我的錢，是信任我判斷能力的朋友，他們的錢」。隨後我們坐了下來喝了些薄荷茶也吃了幾片「甜瓜」。說甜瓜有點言過其實。對他們來說，可以用來招待客人最好的水果就只有黃瓜片了。之前他們選在村裡最好的屋子裡招待我們的，吃的就是這個，現在又來一次。很快我們就將啟程回到通薩，*Jingbi* 隸屬這區域。通薩，位於不丹的南部，離不丹首都廷布六小時車程。通薩堡的建築外觀看似城堡，裡面是寺廟和地區政府的辦公室。

儘管黑山國家公園裡的山丘叢林地形險惡，但是在偏遠的 *Jingbi* 還是收得到手機訊號。我在 *Google* 查「孟巴·不丹」，只跳出了零星的介紹。這裡的孟巴族和西藏南部較大的孟巴族不同，和東印度阿魯納恰爾邦的孟巴族也不同。關於不丹這裡的孟巴族有報導說他們人數還不到四百人，但也有說最多只有六百人的。

探險學會一直都專注在那些具有獨特性的項目，像是在自然和文化領域裡受到忽略或不被重視的，不管是關於人物、動物，或是沒人知道的生態系統。我們像投資者尋找被低估的公司來收購一樣。我們不僅專注大多不為人知的社區，我們也關注不為大多數人所知的國家。大數據和分析對我們的工作沒有什麼用處，對於這些弱勢族群來說，要考慮的有不同的標準。

不丹以國家幸福指數出名，原始的環境、保存良好的宗教聖地、高級的度假村，這裡是「挑剔」的觀光客此生不可錯過的地方。根據當地人類學家 *Seeta Giri* 近二十年前的研究，鮮少人知道的孟巴族如今只剩下不到四百人。但是根據許多資料顯示，孟巴族是喜馬拉雅山脈這裡的原住民，今天正式稱呼是不丹王國，由世襲國王所統治著。

我們這趟就是要更新 *Seeta* 的調查，即便我們的研究方式比較簡單也並非那麼的有系統。首先人口總數就是一個謎題，從四百到六百的調查數字都有，這差異高達百分之五十。但是如果看一下不丹其他的人口統計數字資料，比較過去和現在的資料，或許就可以把謎題解開。

一九七四年出版的美國《國家地理雜誌》，封面故事報導第四任國王的加冕，上面說該國人口有一百一十萬。而今天根據官方的統計，人口才七十萬而已。人口減少的一部分原因是一九九零年超過十萬尼泊爾語族的洛昌人，被迫或自願離開。很明顯的不丹害怕發生隔壁錫金所犯下的前例，那就是，因為外來族群的人口不斷增加，結果在一九七五那年，錫金國變成了印度的一個邦。

一九七四年的人口數字現在漸漸被公認是浮報的，調降了家庭平均所得和個人所得後，讓不丹歸類到貧窮的國家，以至於可以接受世界銀行、聯合國兒童基金會和其他國際組織的更多援助。由此也可以推論，孟巴族的人口是有可能浮報到六百人的。現在的調查方式和交叉檢驗所得到的結果要比以前準確許多了。

我們在 Nidup 的家那裡進行訪問，這是村子裡最好的房子了。好幾位村民，男男女女的擠進客廳，同時也是飯廳兼佛堂，來歡迎我們。Nidup 雖然只有五十三歲，但灰白的捲髮，加上艱困的生活讓他看起來比實際年齡老得多了。Nidup 是當地的釀米酒師也是木匠領班。只要有新屋要蓋的時候，他就會被叫去施工。

訪問進行前有個小儀式，要先唱迎賓歌，並且招待客人喝三輪的米酒。隨後村民一起加入暢快地飲酒。儀式舉行前要先灑一些酒供奉廳裡的神佛。雖然大多數的人信奉佛教，但是村裡還是有一位男的薩滿，有需要的時候會為大家服務。他們端出一碗「水果」招待我們，裡面有幾顆蛋、玉米、香蕉、石榴、甘蔗還有黃瓜。這些都是他們拿得出來最好的東西了。

Nidup 家裡有七位成員。因為孟巴族是母系社會，所以他的母親還保留自己的房子。只有長女才能跟媽媽住，並繼承房子。*Nidup* 與太太共組家庭，家裡有四個小孩還有一位女方那邊的舅舅。老大是個兒子現在在錫金當和尚。老二是女兒，二十三歲，剛跟一位司機結婚，住在女方家，未來會繼承他們的財產。其他小孩，一男一女，結婚後則要自己蓋房子。

Nidup 有六畝地，種兩種農作物，夏天種稻冬天種小麥。他們也種一點玉米和甘蔗。收成時他只能拿一半，因為他的田租給人耕種，耕種的農夫可以拿取一半的收成。田裡也同時種些水果，像是香蕉、木瓜、芒果還有石榴。也養了些家畜，這家人有十頭牛，兩頭乳牛，產下小牛的時候也產乳。因為這家人信奉佛教所以這些牛不會被宰殺。

話題轉回這個村子。這時候有更多的村民加入聊天，回答我的問題。*Jingbi* 村共有二十二戶人家，共一百七十二人。村裡的學校有五十五位學生，其中六位是老師的小孩，老師是政府從外地派來的。另有六位學生是隔壁村的，他們住校，宿舍就在學校旁邊。這所小學從一年級到六年級。學校建於一九九五年，是在第四任國王的舅舅支持下蓋的。自來水在一九九二年才接到這村子裡。因為信仰佛教，年輕男性都可能會出家。在 *Jingbi* 有十二位男性出家，三位尼姑住在尼姑寺。

傳統的竹屋已經都消失了。現在孟巴族住的木造屋，有石頭砌的牆還有金屬屋頂，和一般不丹人住的房子沒什麼區別，只不過沒什麼裝飾，簡樸許多。這些房子都是皇室支持蓋的。幾乎沒有甚麼外來人到這三個孟巴族住的偏遠村子：*Jingbi*、*Wangling* 還有 *Phumzur*。二零零一年才有一條路可以到 *Jingbi*，當地人走兩個鐘頭可以到 *Wangling* 村，但我們可能要花上兩倍的時間才到得了。在這裡，一年有兩個節日，一個在三月還是四月，另一個在十二月十日，節慶時村民聚在一起兩天，他們舉行慶典儀式，飲酒跳舞。

傳統裡孟巴族是獵人也是採集者，熟知民族傳統用植物，知道哪些可以食用哪些可以藥用。不過因為生活型態開始改變，所以這些知識也漸漸失傳了。用蕁麻和大麻莖纖維織布也在漸漸消失。只剩下兩位女性還知道怎麼織這樣的布。我看到 Nidup 的女兒會用手搖織布機，只不過她現在做的是染布紗。在另一戶人家裡我遇到一位女性依舊採收蕁麻，用蕁麻織布。我們找到一件蕁麻做的斗篷，在森林裡揹東西的時候可以用這斗篷來保護背部。這裡到處都生長大麻。徒步時孟巴人順手採了一些新鮮的大麻做成一頂帽子讓我遮擋炎炎烈日。只可惜這頂大麻做的帽子我想帶也帶不走，肯定過不了海關那一關。

孟巴族以往會用有毒的弓箭打獵。兩或三人一組進森林獵捕野豬、熊、鹿、和豪豬，這些在附近山丘常見的動物。偶爾會看到老虎的腳印，但是從來沒捕過。如果打到獵物，每個村民都可以分到一些野味。這裡也有犀鳥。村民都知道公犀鳥會讓母鳥關在樹洞裡生蛋，之後公鳥會帶回食物給母鳥和幼鳥吃。村民從不傷害這些犀鳥。

Bhurba 今年三十二歲，是少數還會打獵的孟巴族。他提議帶我們去他家看怎麼用箭做陷阱，他說去他家只要走十分鐘。沒想到，他的十分鐘變成三十多分鐘，有很多上坡路。每次我問還要走多久的時候，得到的答案總是「就在前面了」。不管是哪一塊大陸的山地部落，好像都用同一方式計算距離和時間對他們來說好像是同義詞。

越過山脊，我們一路穿過了竹林、松樹林還有大麻叢。有間獨立的房子隱藏在樹叢間，沒跟其他村民的房子蓋在一起，那就是 Bhurba 的家。我是團隊裡最後走到的，Bhurba 已經在後院架好陷阱了。看起來就是用木頭把弓箭架在地面上。弓的長度大概超過六呎。拉到底可以承載五十多公斤。

Bhurba 示範了陷阱要怎麼設，以及一旦動物觸動，箭就會發射出去。陷阱設好之後，Bhurba 就得常常會去查看，一個月可能捕到一隻動物。打獵跟採集都已經漸漸消失，年輕人不想要學這樣辛苦的事兒。如果要捕大型的動物，箭頭就要塗上從樹根提煉出來的劇毒。這種毒素或許有醫學或是其他的價值，應該要被好好研究。

當我們回 Jingbi 村的時候，車子在山路盤旋，突然司機停下來指著森林。就在離我們很近的地方，有一群猴子在樹上跳來跳去。當我踏出車外時，Ugyen 告訴我牠們是金葉猴。

我馬上想到兩天前 Ugyen 給我的一本書《不丹的哺乳動物》，就在第九頁有一張黃葉猴的畫像和地圖。書上寫著「不丹人喜歡牠們金色的毛髮和舉止。牠們不會破壞農作物，在路上看到牠們是個吉兆」。

真的，在我們結束拜訪孟巴族的時候看到這些罕見的靈長類動物，的確是個吉兆。

Bhurba's bow & arrow / Bhurba 的弓箭

Monpas weaved objects / 孟巴族的編織物

來自過去的火車

TRAIN FROM
THE PAST

Inle Lake, Myanmar – September 7, 2019

TRAIN FROM THE PAST
Narrow gauge train ride from Shwe Nyaung to Kalaw

"Just watch carefully," I told Sandra, our Myanmar Country Manager. "When the whistle blows and the train starts pulling out, she'll buy some more." Aung Ban is a sizable town and half an hour away is an even bigger town Kalaw, where the lady would likely get off with her merchandise for the market. The platform here is filled with venders of all sorts sitting on the ground with their assortment of vegetables or selling eatables from baskets over their heads while walking along beside the train peddling to passengers.

Sure enough, just as the train started moving, the lady sitting next to us dug out some cash from her purse and passed it out the window. A huge bag of tomatoes came in through the same window just as the train was picking up speed to leave the platform. "Ask her how much cheaper the price is," I told Sandra. The more perishable the goods, the lower the prices would get, as if not sold, it would not last until the next day. It turned out the lady got her tomatoes at half price.

I recall in my National Geographic article in 1984, I described transactions under somewhat opposite circumstances that affected the fluctuation of prices on the high plateau. "In the middle

Tin Tun & Ko Zaw Oo

of Qinghai Lake lies a tiny island once occupied by a Tibetan monastery. Songs of the children of Xining used to recount how in winter the lamas walked across the frozen surface of the lake to shore to sell their handmade goods and buy daily necessities. As spring approached, the lamas sighed in grief as the merchants, who were mostly Muslims, raised their prices on the merchandise. They knew that the lamas had to stock up for summer and rush back to their island before the ice thawed."

In the case of the train ride, the lady insisted that I had taken up her seat by the window, obviously the most conducive to last minute transactions. I moved across the aisle and seated myself across from an elderly lady, who was busily using a knife to open the hard shells of a bushel of dogfruit, or jengkol, quickly pulling out the white soft inner fruits and tossing them into another basket. It is said that selling just the inside naked without the shell would yield five times the price. I joked with Sandra that this is synonymous with the sex industry, and she seemed annoyed by my comparison.

Sandra on scenic ride / Sandra 搭乘風景優美的火車

The lady who occupied my seat introduced herself as Daw Tin Ngwe, a Pa'o (a hilltribe) from Shwe Taw, or Golden Village. She has her own small stall there selling snacks and groceries. The luggage with her, all fresh vegetables like cabbage and melons, had totally taken up the upper luggage racks, as well as the seat next to and across from her. From the way she interacted with the venders, she must do this round all the time.

Illustrating her point by stretching her arms fully, Daw Tin Ngwe bragged to Sandra that her prices will go up multiple times by the time the goods reach market. Furthermore, she need not buy a passenger ticket, but only pays for her cargo while taking the "upper" class, which had cost us 1200 Kyat (less than US$1), rather than "regular", which costs only 100 Kyat. Surely a deal has been made with the conductor, who strolled by occasionally, covering the four passenger carriages with two additional goods carriages way in the back. His may be a lucrative job to have, since the train is almost full with paid and unpaid passengers.

While waiting at the starting station at Shwe Nyaung, ten kilometers from Inle Lake, we chatted with the station manager as well as the train engineer. Today, tear-off tickets are still handwritten. U Tin Tun is 56 years old, and was engineer/driver of the train for 25 years before being promoted to become the station manager. His young protégé, now driving the train, is Ko Zaw Oo. On any regular day, they may start with 25 or so passengers, but the number would grow as the train made stops at other onward stations. By the time it pulled out of Aung Ban, the train would be largely full, well before reaching Kalaw.

The entire ride this morning from Shwe Nyaung to Kalaw would take about three hours, starting at 8am. But the long stop at Aung Ban for an hour made this daily trip a four-hour ordeal. If fresh milk had been one of the cargoes, by the time we reached Kalaw we would have had our milk shake ready for serving. This is a well-known roller coaster experience for a train ride in Myanmar, especially so for the narrow-gauge train that runs on tracks that are one meter wide, about half that of the regular six-foot wide tracks.

It is said that the country still has over 5000 kilometers of narrow-gauge tracks. On our route, a diesel engine has replaced the old steam one, though I heard that, in some of the distant routes in the logging region to the north, steam is still being used. This would be a great opportunity for train enthusiasts and aficionados.

Ready to eat vendor / 販賣熟食的攤販

Platform at Aung Ban / 安邦的月台

From the start, the train went through some wonderful rural scenery, patches of green rice paddies, yellow rape seed fields, red pre-planting earth, or ripe green and newly harvested gray cornfields. Today, almost no train rides in the developed world offer open windows where fresh air comes rushing in. On this ride, even trees and plants, not trimmed, came brushing inside the cabin. Passengers must be careful not to lean out and endanger head or arms.

About half an hour into the ride, the train began climbing. By an hour, after skirting the sides of hills, the train did a circular climb to higher elevation, crossing a bridge looking down onto the tracks we had just passed earlier. This section offered a grand view of the entire valley that made up the Inle Lake region before we got to the higher plain of Heho where the airport is located. The air became obviously cooler. At one point, the train stopped in the middle of nowhere. The engine stalled, but a quick repair got us going after about ten minutes. For other passengers, as well as the train conductor, such stoppings seemed rather routine.

Tin Ngwe with both seats / Tin Ngwe 占用兩個座位
Upper Class passenger / 升等座位的乘客
Vender inside carriage / 車廂內的攤販

Finally at about noon, we reached Kalaw four hours after leaving Shwe Nyaung. The town was a former hill station for the British to get away from the scorching summer heat of the plains. There are many colonial style houses, which have become a feature for tourists. We stopped in one such house that has been turned into the Seven Sisters, a fine restaurant. The seven sisters had turned old age and away. While the cuisine is definitely Burmese/Shan, the bottle of wine from Red Mountain Vineyard boasted a French ancestry, as the founder/owner is of French descent.

For the return trip, we opted for a van, which took us back to our CERS base at Inle Lake in less than three hours. But the one-day excursion on a historic train ride was certainly worthwhile. And the observation of market manipulation and speculation on the train was an excellent case study, little different from the sharks of Wall Street. Only, in scale, this one was a minnow.

Seven Sisters Restaurant / 七姐妹餐館

Fruit market in Kalaw / 格勞的水果市場

來自過去的火車

從娘瑞坐窄軌火車到格勞

「仔細看著！」我跟我們緬甸的項目經理 Sandra 說。「當汽笛作響，火車開始移動的時候，她就會再多買一些。」安邦是蠻大的城鎮，半小時車程遠的格勞是個更大的城市，那位女士會在那裡帶著她的商品下車到市場去賣。月台上滿滿的都是賣東西的小販，他們在地上擺滿各種蔬菜，或是把食物裝在籃子裡頂在頭上在月台上跟乘客兜售。

不出意外，就當火車開始動的時候，坐在我們旁邊的女士從錢包裡拿出一些錢遞出窗口。火車開始加速離開月台時一大袋的番茄從窗戶送進來。「問問她這袋便宜了多少？」我跟 Sandra 說。越容易壞掉的蔬果便越折價，因為這些賣不了的蔬果隔天就不能賣了。果然那袋番茄只要了半價。

我想起一篇一九八四年我為美國《國家地理雜誌》寫的文章，文章描述那時在高原上的狀況跟此刻恰好相反，內容跟高原上的物價波動有關。「青海湖中有個很小的小島，上面有個藏傳寺廟。西寧小孩唱的兒歌，述說寒冬中的喇嘛走過結冰的湖面到岸上去販賣他們自己做的東西，然後購買一些日常必需品。當春天快要來到的時候，喇嘛悲傷地嘆氣，那些販賣商品的穆斯林商人又要哄抬價錢了。因為他們知道喇嘛必須要在冰湖溶化前採買夏季的必需品趕回寺廟」。

Train climbing / 爬升中的火車

火車上的那位女士堅持說我佔了她靠窗的位子，明明就是想要方便自己買東西罷了。我索性換到走道另一邊的座位，坐在一位大嬸的對面，那位大嬸正忙著用刀把臭豆從豆莢裡挖出來，並熟練地把白色的豆子丟到另一個籃子裡去。據說脫掉豆莢的豆子可以賣到比整個豆莢高出五倍的價錢。我開玩笑地跟 *Sandra* 說這不就跟性產業一樣，她好像不太高興我用這樣的比喻。

佔我座位的女士介紹自己叫 *Daw Tin Ngwe*，巴奧族，來自 *Shwe Taw* 又稱黃金村。她在村子裡有個賣零食和雜貨小攤子。她的行李塞滿了座位上面的行李架，也佔用了隔壁還有對面的座上，她的行李全都是新鮮的蔬果像是高麗菜跟甜瓜。從她跟賣家的互動看來，她一定經常都是這樣。

她伸直了手臂來強調她的言談內容，她跟 *Sandra* 炫耀說這些東西到了市場就會漲個好幾倍。此外，她還不用買車票，只需要付行李的費用就好了，她佔用我們用一千兩百緬元（不到一美金）買的「升等」座位，而普通座位只需要一百緬元。她一定是跟車長有默契！車長負責四節乘客的車廂跟兩節在後面的貨車廂，車長會不定時在車廂內走動。他的工作應該很有賺頭，因為車上坐滿了買車票跟沒買車票的乘客。

起點的娘瑞車站離茵萊湖十公里，趁著等車的時候我們跟站長還有火車的工程師聊天。直到現在車票還要用手撕的，也還是用手寫的。五十六歲的 *U Tin Tun* 當了二十五年的工程師兼駕駛後被提升為站長。他的徒弟 *Ko Zaw Oo* 現在負責開火車。平日在起點差不多會有二十五位乘客，每停一站就會有更多乘客上車，到安邦後火車就差不多坐滿了，從安邦到格勞還有一段距離。

早上八點從娘瑞坐到格勞要三個鐘頭。但是光在安邦就停留了一個鐘頭，導致旅程變成煎熬的四個鐘頭。如果新鮮的牛奶在貨車上，到格勞的時候應該已經變成奶昔了。在緬甸坐火車就像在坐雲霄飛車，尤其是只有一公尺寬的窄軌火車，大約是一般六呎寬軌道的一半。

據說緬甸有超過五千公里長的窄軌。我們坐的火車已經不再用蒸氣引擎而換成柴油引擎了，但是我聽說有些北部的筏木區還有蒸氣引擎的火車。鐵道迷應該會很想來試試看才對。

從起點開始，火車經過景色很漂亮的鄉間，綠油油的稻田，黃澄澄的油菜田，剛整好地的紅土，成熟的玉米田和剛收割的田地。在已開發的地方搭火車，幾乎不可能開窗讓新鮮的空氣吹進來。但是這趟旅程有些路段還有一些樹和植物被打進車廂內，乘客

Repair stop / 停下來修火車

Hot food vender / 熱食攤販

可要小心不要把頭太靠近窗邊，要不然可會被打到。

火車開了半個鐘頭之後開始爬坡。一個鐘頭後開始繞著山丘爬升，當火車跨過一條橋的時候往下看，可以看到我們剛剛經過的地方就在腳下。這一段剛好可以看到整個茵萊湖區的山谷，再往前就是海拔更高的平原 — 黑河，機場就座落在這裏。這裡的空氣明顯地變得比較冷。一度火車的引擎不動了，停在前不著村後不著店的地方。還好差不多十分鐘就修好了。車長和其他乘客對這樣的狀況似乎都不以為意。

從娘瑞出發四個鐘頭之後，我們終於在中午到了格勞。這城市以前是英國人來避暑的山站。有許多殖民時代的房子現在變成觀光景點。我們去了一家叫「七姊妹」的高級餐廳，就是其中之一。七姐妹已經老去，料理是道地的緬甸菜，還有法國血統的紅山葡萄園的葡萄酒，因為創辦人和老闆是法國裔。

回程我們選擇廂型車載我們回到探險學會在茵萊湖的基地，整趟路程不到三個鐘頭。不過坐這樣有歷史的火車一日遊還是很值得的。在火車上可以觀察到市場是被如何操作的、投機份子是怎麼運作的，跟華爾街的鯊魚有些許不同，但不同的只是規模的差別，在這裡操縱市場的，看來還只是條小魚兒呢。

Regular class / 普通艙
Dogfruit lady & seat hogger / 挑臭豆的女士和佔位者

束埔寨和越南的邊境城市

BORDER TOWN OF
CAMBODIA WITH VIETNAM

Kep, Cambodia – September, 2019

barely two inches across. It turned out the big crab had long ago been decimated. All the fishermen who set out to sea could only get tiny ones these days. Overfishing is taking its toll.

The following morning, we went to the nearby Kep Market. Tropical fruits were plentiful and I bought some Lung An and a pomelo. The Cambodians are a pretty lot and I could not stop choosing some nice portraits on which to aim my camera. Just a short distance from the market is the small fishing village of Kep. At a house by the ocean, I met Kim. She was formerly a tour guide and was housesitting for a French boating tour owner who was on vacation back home. Her husband and mother-in-law had joined her at the house.

In the courtyard, mother-in-law had spread out a big netted sheet, on which were drying some tiny silver shrimps. This was for the making of her own allotment of shrimp sauce. "You know why we make our own? Those you buy in market are mass produced. While drying, the flies get on it and maybe lay baby flies," Kim said with all seriousness on her face. I asked and begged, and finally was able to purchase two jars with about four kilos of this home-made shrimp sauce.

"I know coastal Southeast Asia has a lot of ancient Muslim communities. Are there any near Kep?" I asked Kim. "Yes, there are two villages nearby, between Kep and Kampong," answered Kim. Before long, I was on my way in a tuktuk heading to

Evening bather / 傍晚泡在水裡的人們

Phone shot / 用手機拍照
Family selfie / 一家人自拍
Looking out from Sailing Club / 從帆船俱樂部看出去

Krong Kaeb village. We arrived at the mosque some twenty minutes out of Kep, just in time to observe the noon service. About thirty or so Muslims were starting to converge outside, washing themselves and beginning to file into the very new looking building.

They were wondering why we had come, and one young man walked up to question me. I sat up, knowing Muslims could be a rather closed society, always a bit apprehensive of outsiders. From my mobile phone, I quickly Googled "Islamic Frontiers of China," a book I authored back in 1990. I showed him my phone image to prove that I am a friend of Islam. This brought forth a welcoming smile, and we managed to chat a little, just before he had to go inside the Masjid Phum Sbov Mosque.

He told me that most of the villagers are fishermen and farmers nearby. He had been to Mecca just a year ago and now has the title of Haji, conferred only to those who have made that pilgrimage. He said that, this year, about twenty from their two villages had gone. Now, more and more could afford to make the pilgrimage as families become more wealthy with

Gold store money exchanger / 在金飾店兌換貨幣
Sundry vender / 雜貨店家
Fruit vender / 水果攤販

better income, since tourism has been on the rise.

As the sound of chanting was picking up from a microphone inside the clean hall, we took a brief look at the cemetery outside the mosque and continued on our journey. But now, it was lunch time and we were near the Kep Sailing Club, somewhat like a British type of yacht club. Lounging by the ocean with a drink in hand, I waited for our order of fish & chips.

With the blue crab gone, obviously there is no conflict of interest even if we start a project here. Tomorrow, I should cross the border and explore the Vietnamese side. Perhaps there, I would find my blue crab. After all, having a project base there would also benefit Kep here on the Cambodian side. Now, I call that complementary interest!

Village Mosque / 村里的清真寺
Muslim villagers / 穆斯林村民

Service inside Mosque / 清真寺裡的禮拜

柬埔寨和越南的邊境城市

螃蟹不見了

我的座位在 48J，空中巴士 320 的最後一排，靠窗的座位，洗手間就在後面。下飛機時我會是最後一個，除非有緊急狀況發生，座位靠後面的緊急逃生出口離我最近。抵達金邊國際機場過海關時我很自然的就是排在最後的人。

當你排在最後面的時候可以冒一些風險，反正沒什麼好損失的。我走向 APEC 櫃台拿出我的 APEC 卡，看看可不可以快速通關，即便卡片背面列出一堆環太平洋國家，卻沒列進柬埔寨。我推測海關根本懶得看背面寫些什麼。海關如果讓我通關的話，我就會是第一個出機場，去飯店。如果海關注意到我的卡片是無效的，我頂多就是說聲抱歉然後回到隊伍的最後面，繼續排隊。反正也不會嚴重到被判刑。

這趟我的目的地是白馬，介於越南和柬埔寨。回到金邊，不僅我順利快速通關，連跟著我的兩個同事也是。海關根本沒檢視 APEC 卡，只是看了一眼就放在櫃台上。

即使暴雨下下停停，我仍然在湄公河旁的柬埔寨飯店過了愉快的一夜。有幾次我們騎著電動三輪車去市中心吃飯。這裡雖然沒有那麼靠近印度，但是卻有很多印度餐飲店。酒吧和酒吧女郎一路從越南、泰國邊界進入柬埔寨，算是一九六零年代東南亞美軍基地的副產品。

Mekong outside Cambodiana Hotel / 從柬埔寨飯店看出去的湄公河

隔天早上我們租了一台休旅車，從金邊開到位在海邊的白馬需要四個多鐘頭，離越南邊界大約二十公里。我對白馬市的興趣並沒有什麼奇特。我常常用地圖來看看哪裡是最高回報和最適合我們著手新項目的地方。實地勘察後，如果我喜歡這個地方，我不會介意為了這項目常常回來－ *Bingo*！

根據我們現在在南亞和東南亞的項目，我想要在政治上敏感的南海一帶多找一個點，看看有沒有可能做的事。這樣的地方會更有趣，儘管會更有挑戰性。白馬吸引了我的注意。如果我們在那裏有個基地，然後在地圖上插上探險學會的旗子，那麼旗子應該會橫跨兩個國家。這樣會比較有利。

政府正在蓋一條四線道路從首都到貢布和施亞努市，那裏是白馬附近的觀光休閒度假區。道路修好後前往那裏的時間就會縮短一半。我們的司機三十一歲，結了婚有兩個小孩，他很驕傲的跟我說他的祖父是中國人，跟一個當地人結婚。所以他也會說一些中文。他說施亞努市的海濱有很多來自中國的有錢人，買下好多新建的海灘別墅跟公寓。但是這對我來說一點吸引力都沒有。

我還記得曾在網路上搜尋白馬的照片，然而吸引我的不是海灘和藍海，而是一隻很大的藍蟹，牠被海水圍繞著，還有個牌子寫著「歡迎來到白馬」。如果我們選在白馬做事，可能會有利益衝突的問題。因為我很喜歡螃蟹，特別是藍蟹。別管這了，柬埔寨語的白馬跟英文的螃蟹聽起來很像，或許其他人不會注意到。

到白馬後我們住進 Riviera 飯店，還不到兩年的新飯店只有八間房，老闆是 Sovanna Khim 和她的先生。他們第一次來白馬就愛上這裡，於是放下家鄉的三個事業讓別人去管理。身為法國人，很自然地用 Riviera 當作飯店的名字。如果這個地方可以抓住浪漫的法國人，那就不必用太多文字來形容了。

雖然已經接近傍晚，但是還是有很多人在外面閒逛。柬埔寨正在慶祝為期三天的國慶日。路上有好多放在摩托推車檯子上的小吃可以選擇，各式各樣的小吃。我喝了最受歡迎的甘蔗汁，很多攤都有榨甘蔗機。我們還買了炸栗子和榴槤，鄰近的貢布是柬埔寨最大的榴槤產地。我不敢接近榴槤，但是我們一位組員可是愛死了榴槤，我則是怕死了榴槤。

好多人跟水岸邊的雕像自拍，有些也會跟家人一起自拍。儘管太陽漸漸下山，接近傍晚了，還是有很多人泡在水裡。附近海灘的簡便淋浴設施是用桶子或是大型塑膠容器搭建。整條海岸擠滿了前來慶祝的人、車、小攤、和帳篷，一直到入夜後還是很熱鬧。

Durian peddler / 榴槤攤販
Sugarcane cart / 甘蔗汁車
Motorized food cart / 摩托車上的小吃攤販

我們想要走去螃蟹市場，那裡面有三十幾家海鮮餐廳。當地人說只要二十幾分鐘到半個鐘頭就可以到。可是過了一個鐘頭，天早已經黑了，我們還沒走到。好不容易看到一台嘟嘟車，我招了下來，開了十五分鐘才到。我們選了一家有最多活海鮮的餐廳，我的首選當然是那個大藍蟹，結果店家只拿得出來很小的，才不到兩吋大。原來大螃蟹早就被捕光了，漁民現在出海只能捕到小隻的。過度捕撈可是要付出代價的。

隔天早上我們到旁邊的白馬市場。市場有很多熱帶水果，我買了一些龍眼和一顆柚子。我打算選幾個人拍人像，但是柬埔寨人個個都長得很好看，我的相機快門幾乎無法停下。離白馬不遠的地方有個小漁村。在一間靠海的房子我碰到了 Kim。她以前是位導遊，現在正在幫一位法國遊艇公司的老闆看房子，老闆正回家度假。Kim 的先生和婆婆也一起來陪她看房子。

Kim 的婆婆在院子裡鋪了一張網，網上曬著小銀蝦，用來做她自己的蝦醬。「你知道為什麼我們要自己做嗎？你在市場上買的都是大量生產的。日曬時蒼蠅會飛進去產卵，裡面還會有小蒼蠅！」

Kim 很嚴肅地說。我不斷地拜託，她才願意賣給我兩罐自製蝦醬，大約四公斤重。

「我知道東南亞有很多古老的穆斯林社區。白馬附近有嗎？」我問 Kim。「有啊，有兩個，就在白馬和甘榜中間。」Kim 回答。沒過多久，我就坐上了嘟嘟車前往 Krong Kaeb 村。離白馬二十分鐘，我們在中午抵達清真寺，剛好是中午禱告的時間。大約三十幾位穆斯林聚集在外面，正在淨身，準備排隊進入這棟看起來很新的建築物。

他們對我們的出現感到好奇，有個年輕人走過來問我。我坐直身體，我知道穆斯林有點封閉，對外人也比較有警覺性。用我的手機快速 Google 了《Islamic Frontier of China》中國邊境穆斯林這本我在一九九零年代寫的書。他看了後給了我微笑，我們小聊了一下，然後他就進去 Masjid Phum Sbov 清真寺。

Mobile shop / 摩托車小店　　　　　　　　　　　　　　Shopping cart / 百貨推車

他跟我說附近的村民多是漁夫和農民。他一年前去過麥加，已經是哈吉，這是授予朝聖者的稱號。他說今年村子裡大約有二十位村民也去朝聖。拜蓬勃的觀光產業所賜，現在家庭收入比以往好得多了，越來越多人有能力可以去朝聖。

麥克風裡的頌禱聲從潔淨的大廳傳來，看了一下清真寺外面的墓園後我們繼續行程。午餐時間到了，而我們正走在白馬帆船俱樂部附近，這裡感覺很像英國的遊艇俱樂部。等待炸魚和薯條上桌的同時，我手上拿著酒在海邊晃悠著。

既然藍蟹已經不見了，那麼我們在這裡開始項目也不會有利益衝突了。明天我會跨過邊境去越南探險，也許可以在那裏找到我的藍蟹。如果在那邊有個項目其實也會對柬埔寨這邊的白馬有利。我稱之為互利。

House by ocean / 海邊的房屋

往上游去，再出海去

UP THE RIVER,
OUT THE OCEAN

Ha Tien, Vietnam – October 3, 2019

UP THE RIVER, OUT THE OCEAN
Exploring Vietnam southernmost coast

The peace and tranquility can be misleading. The Patrol Craft Fast (PCF), also known as a "swift boat," was speeding up the Giang Thanh river canal from the coastal village of Ha Tien. Both banks of the river were lined with mangrove and palm trees, with an occasional open area where you could see the rice paddy beyond. A few thatched huts, serving as isolated abodes for fishermen or farmers, dotted the otherwise barren landscape.

The Giang Thanh is a river that on and off divides the border of Cambodia with Vietnam. The border is neither well defined nor demarcated, at times fluctuating as the river changes course over decades or centuries, thus making the border as murky as the sediment-filled river water. It is sometimes difficult to know when you are in one country, and when in the other. In such remote areas, peasants cross back and forth, so it seems the border is only symbolic. But like the swift boats heading up river, politics can swiftly turn such an area into a hot spot. Hot spot indeed it once was, as those same armored boats had flamethrowers that could burn down the brush, and the houses, within seconds.

On that day however, what seemed peaceful was just the calm before the storm. It was around Christmas 1968, and a small corps of three swift boats, each fifty feet in length, were dispatched upstream looking for trouble, or to subdue those who wanted to inflict trouble. The boats had machine guns front and aft, as well as grenade/rocket launchers amidships. A turret on the top was capable of discharging incendiary napalm, a flamethrower artillery that could burn the trees and shrubs along the bank to expose any potential danger of ambush from the enemy. The napalm was made more toxic by the addition of a magnesium agent, so that when a person was in flames and jumped into the river, the water would make the flames burn even more fiercely.

The soldiers on these boats were nicknamed "riverines", also known as the Brown Water Navy. Just like marines, they were a cross between the Army and Navy, except that they operated on rivers – especially rivers in the delta of the Mekong. Sometimes the boats were on regular patrol. Other times they might be dropping off a Navy Seal, or covert personnel attached to the CIA operatives in Vietnam, as they would penetrate beyond the left bank of the river border into Cambodia, a country which was proclaimed neutral in which America never declared a war zone, but which was infested with the VC, or Vietcong.

On this day, one of the gunboats was led by a young man, John Kerry, who would later become a US senator, and then a Presidential candidate, narrowly losing in his campaign against George W. Bush, and then later serving as Secretary of State under the Obama Administration. That early river patrol mission would in time be casted into the forefront of US election politics, becoming an issue that haunted John Kerry's presidential campaign. "Swiftboating" would also become a new addition to the political lexicon, synonymous to a smear campaign, after the 2004 Kerry presidential bid.

It all involved several military medals, a Purple Heart for injury inflicted in action, a Bronze and a Silver for other military valor, which Kerry received for his time on this river. It derived from several engagements that drew exchange of fire and artillery between the Vietcong and the US military's Swift Boats. As a Vietnam veteran who spoke out against the war in 1971, Kerry made more than a few enemies, Republicans in particular, who would later turn against him during his presidential campaign.

During other incidents on this same river, exchange of fire would at times require military inquiry about whether officers had adhered to engagement protocol, which if broken, might result in a court martialing. In reality, any actions taken were more for show than for real effect. The book Swift Boat at War in Vietnam documents and narrates such activities and outcomes vividly.

The author's unauthorized action, gunning a boat crossing with civilians in the vicinity, triggered a serious objection and protest from Prince Sihanouk, leader of independent Cambodia at the time. The US soldier involved claimed his action was justified because he was in "hot pursuit," returning gunfire from someone on the left bank. Hot pursuit meant that, if you were in close visible contact with the enemy and exchanging fire, you could disregard boundaries until the firing ceased. In short, this was a hot river fifty years ago.

My cruise up the same river is very peaceful, though it brought back memories of what I had read about a more turbulent time. It was a time when I had just entered college in America, thus being caught up in the campus anti-war mayhem of the time. Several of my friends were veterans returning from Vietnam and attending college under the GI Bill.

It was six o'clock this morning when we waited for the boat that we had ordered yesterday. It was supposed to be waiting by the River Hotel, fronting the Giang Thanh River. Ha Tien has morphed from a coastal village in the Delta, to a town, and now a small city. In the mid-1600s, when the Ming Dynasty fell to the Manchu, a Chinese by the name of Mac Cuu, a loyalist from Guangdong, came here to hide from the newly installed Qing court. The then king of Annam (Vietnam today) gave the area to Mac Cuu. Today a temple-cum-mausoleum still exists to pay tribute to this earliest of settlers.

Today, the highest building in town is the River Hotel where we are staying. Other tall buildings, almost similar in height to ours, are mostly without windows, much like warehouses. Yet some may have balconies and villa-like-

Temple of Cambodia across border / 過邊境的柬埔寨寺廟

Upper floors for swiftlets / 高樓層給金絲燕

façades, just for decoration. A few use the lower floors as home, with the upper floors looking like factory warehouses.

The houses, however, are not for people or dry goods, but for attracting the hundreds of thousands of swiftlets. They live by the coast where limestone hills and islands have for centuries provided caves and cavities for nesting birds. Now their needs are served by these avian condominiums. High atop the roofs on poles are perched small loudspeakers, broadcasting tweet-like sounds resembling swiftlet flocks, thus attracting the birds inside the buildings to make nests. These swiftlet's songs are tweeted out all day long, even into the night, perhaps just as Trump sends out his morning and evening tweets.

Collection of such nests, formerly in the wild and now in part from those birds harnessed for harvest indoor, is an age-old tradition. Composed of excretions in the saliva of the birds, the nests will be refined and sorted. The finished bird nest products, ranging in colors from white to yellow to even red, are believed to be of extremely high value as a health supplement. Top quality bird nests are said to fetch upwards of $10,000 USD per kilo. Around Ha Tien, many of the richer families conduct such lucrative business.

Our boat is a narrow long-tailed boat around eighteen feet in length. There are five rows of bench seats, each just fit for one person. Chartering it for a four hour ride cost us $30 USD, or a few pints worth of bird nests. As we sail upriver, it is day and night from what I read about the patrol boat going up the Giang Thanh some fifty years ago. Twenty minutes upriver there is a village by the bank. Many houses still have thatched roofs with straw sidings, while the more affluent ones may be brick or cement, and a few are hybrids with both straw and brick. It seems boats are the main transport means, as these narrow boats are prevalent everywhere. Almost all are now made of fiberglass. During the entire morning, I see only two wooden long boats, and a few dilapidated bigger wooden junks.

Once beyond a village, there are many mangroves and palms, but few coconut trees. Waterfowl abound, like egrets, cormorants and an occasional kingfisher. As we move upriver, the houses immediately became much fewer and are scattered far apart. Interestingly, trees and palms along the banks are left mostly intact. In the past, such forests probably stretched into the distance. But today, beyond the first row of trees, one can see the paddy fields

Mac Cuu's temple / 供奉鄭玖的廟

Tourist tricycle / 載觀光客的三輪車

with dikes right behind. Cutting down the trees for farming may seem socially and economically equitable for a largely agrarian society, but surely is not environmentally sound.

There are a couple of times when our young boat driver Khrung wants to take us into side channels, but each time I insist on staying in the main river. After all, we don't want to be ambushed by any remnants of the Vietnam War. With the map on my phone, I want to trace the river as it meanders to where it is closest to, or overlaps with, the national border with Cambodia.

At a spot where my map shows me that we were right at the border, I ask Khrung to pull to the left bank where a rusted metal shed stands. I want to find out whether the family living in it is Cambodian or Vietnamese. Jing turns out to be a farmer. He and his wife with three buffaloes and a few ducks eke out a basic living here.

I point to the high pinnacle roof of a distant temple and ask Jing whether I can go there. He shakes his head and says that is inside Kampuchea, meaning Cambodia. Around 500 meters away from the bank are a few houses. Those are also inside Cambodia. We discuss taking a walk over, like I often do when crossing remote national borders. Xavier, our filmmaker, cautions me that there might be mine fields around. I think for a second, and acquiesce.

As I get back on our boat and say goodbye to Jing, I suddenly remember my own admonishment to young adults. "You have seen the place, but has the place seen you?" "Try to leave an impact, little as it may be," I often tell them. From my carrying bag, I take out a bag of cooked chestnuts, and ask Xavier to pass it over to Jing. With a big smile on both of our faces, my boat starts downstream again. As the trees and the villagers gradually move behind me, they blend into the peaceful landscape. That is a far cry from the scourge of the patrol boat that sped up and down the river fifty years ago.

A few years after John Kerry was in Vietnam, on April 30, 1975, just as the first tank rolled into Saigon (now Ho Chi Minh City) and an Air America Huey helicopter evacuated the last Americans from the rooftop of a building, the Cambodian Khmer Rouge Army prepared to make a daring move to capture Phu Quoc, an island off Ha Tien. This was the largest island within Vietnam, and was presumably then still under the South Vietnam regime.

Historically, Phu Quoc belonged to either Vietnam or Cambodia, depending on which of the two countries was stronger. Though Vietnam occupied it during much of the 20th century, Cambodia continued to claim it. The Khmer Rouge took the island on May 1, 1975, but soon the liberating Army of Vietnam retook Phu Quoc. The on-and off friction between the two communist countries continued until 1979, when Vietnam intruded into Cambodia and began an occupation that lasted for almost ten years before they retreated and established détente and relative stability.

We wanted to visit the island for a very different reason. I had heard that the very best fish sauce in the world comes from Phu Quoc, especially the 45°N pure vintage that requires the anchovies to "ferment" in brine inside huge wood and rattan barrels two to four meters in height. The resulting product is said to be quite blissful to some, and repulsive to others. A Vietnamese author once noted that old fishermen would down a cup of this sauce just to keep warm before a long journey out to sea, and divers likewise would toast with it before taking a plunge into the cold ocean. The vintage is even compared to French wine and Italian olive oil.

We boarded the ferry at 6am, and, after an hour and a half in a hydrofoil, we landed at a jetty at the eastern coast of Phu Quoc Island. Hiring a taxi for seven hours, costing us a meager $30 USD, we headed for the bottom tip of the island. Near the fishing harbor and town of An Thoi is a company called Phung Hung that specializes in the fish sauce. Once I got out of the car at the parking lot, a pungent smell struck me. That smell filled the air for the next hour as I strolled the grounds, the factory, and the shops within the premises of the company.

Of course, the most spectacular was the open-air factory lined with huge drums for fermentation. It is said that the wood for making these drums is special, only from the island, and it is becoming so rare that no more such trees are allowed to be felled. The reddish-brown color of the barrels is also quite exceptional, somehow complementing the smell of the fermented fish sauce. Three parts

Fish arriving port / 漁獲到港

Squid & Cuttlefish / 烏賊

of anchovies and one part of brine is the formula for the concoction that results in a special sauce, the fermentation of which can take a year or two to complete. In addition to anchovy, sardine and mackerel can also be used, but that would make the cost much higher.

Cleaning / 清理漁獲

At the shop, I met Kim, manager for the owner family. She introduced me to several varieties of their brand of fish sauce. The slightly lower grade starts from 30° to 40°, toping at 45°N. The N stands for nitrogen, and the higher its content, the more pure and pungent the sauce will be. Generally, any 45°N grade would come from the first distillation of the sauce, before more brine is added for distillation and the lower grade yielded. Dipping a tiny straw into a sauce pan, I was invited to taste the high grade sauce. I choked upon my first sip as my throat suddenly tightened into some kind of a contraction. It was as if my seven-decade-old palate and taste buds had come back alive.

Soon I left the shop with two cases of the Phung Hung fish sauce. The tiny bottles, in liquor sampling sizes, would be dispensed as gifts to quench the curiosity of some of my more adventurous friends. I, in turn, must admit to being intoxicated, and possibly somewhat addicted, by this very special taste. The shop had to double-wrap my prized trophies, as it is said that if the bottles are broken on the airplane, it would be considered a criminal *offence, not unlike bringing durian onto a plane.*

I next visited the fishing port at the tip of An Thoi, just in time to see loads of fish being unloaded from boats to shore. Obviously fishing is still a mainstay of the economy of Phu Quoc, though tourism is now fast developing, with beach hotels and resorts sprouting on the island's coast. The airport has recently become an international destination, with flights coming in from Bangkok.

I make it back to the jetty just in time to catch the last ferry, which leaves Phu Quoc back to Ha Tien at 3:30pm. My turnaround is necessarily short. I do not want to repeat the experience of the Chinese Nationalist Army, when, in 1949, the Kuomintang of Chiang Kai-shek retreated to Taiwan. Some 30,000 troops were pushed out of China into Vietnam, and ended up in Phu Quoc. They were stranded here on the island for three years before finally being repatriated to Taiwan by the French in 1953. I, however, have had less than a day, but have had a wonderful sampling of the island, including the best fish sauce in the world.

As I board the ferry, in my pocket is a tiny bottle of Phung Hung fish sauce. In the event that I get seasick, I will take a sip, to stabilize or intoxicate myself!

Happy Ending Phu Quoc / 富國島上美好的結局

往上游去，再出海去

探險越南最南端的海岸

不要被這裡的寧靜給誤導了。快艇巡邏隊 PCF，又稱「快艇」，正從河仙市加速前往江城運河上游。河岸兩邊佈滿了紅樹林和棕櫚樹，透過樹與樹的空隙還可以看到後面的稻田。荒蕪的岸邊蓋了幾間茅草屋，供附近的漁民和農夫使用。

江城河穿梭在柬埔寨和越南的邊境，一下在柬埔寨，一下又在越南。其實兩國的邊界一直沒有被界定清楚，隨著河道幾十年幾百年來的改變，邊界就像充滿泥沙的河水一樣模糊，有時候你根本不知道現在到底在越南還是柬埔寨。在這種偏遠的地區，人們來來回回地跨越邊境，說「邊境」似乎也只是個象徵而已。不過就像快艇衝向上游一樣，政治上的變化也可能讓這種區域提升為衝突的熱點。這裡的確曾經是熱點，裝甲船甚至都還配有噴火器，在幾秒鐘之內就可以燒毀叢林、房子。

那天看似平靜，其實卻是暴雨前的寧靜。一九六八年聖誕節左右，由三艘長達五十五呎的快艇所組成的隊伍，被派去上游找麻煩，另一個說法是，去制伏想找麻煩的人。每艘船的船頭與船尾都配置了機關槍，船身還有手榴彈和火箭發射器。上面的旋轉槍架還可以發射凝固汽油彈，噴火器可以瞬間燒毀沿岸的樹、叢林，讓敵人無處可躲。為了讓汽油彈更具毒性，還加了鎂，當人被火燒到的時候就算跳進水裡也沒用，因為水只會讓火燒的更猛烈。

軍人暱稱這些快艇為「河濱艦隊」，一如褐水海軍。就像海軍陸戰隊那樣，結合了陸軍和海軍，只是他們是在河裡運作，特別是在湄公河三角洲。船隻有時會進行日常的巡邏。有時候也會載海豹突擊隊，或是在越南工作的 CIA 秘密人員，他們會穿越左岸的邊界進入柬埔寨。那時這裡為中立國，美國也沒宣稱這裡是戰區，但是這裡卻有非常多的越共。

這一天年輕時的約翰・克里帶領一艘砲艇出任務，他後來成為美國參議員也曾是總統候選人，以些微的差距輸給布希，他在歐巴馬任期內出任國務卿一職。當克里競選總統的時候，他年輕時在這些河域執行的巡邏任務變成了困擾他的問題。「快艇了」一詞在二零零四年克里競選總統後也變成新的政治用語和動詞，意思是抹黑。

克里在這裡的表現讓他得到紫心勳章，這是頒發給參戰時負傷的人員，他還獲頒銅星以及銀星勳章以表揚他的英勇，表揚他在美軍快艇隊和越共交戰過程中出色的表現。作為越南退伍軍人的他曾在一九七一年表態反對戰爭，因而樹立不少敵人，尤其是共和黨在競選期間更成為了他的敵人。

在這條河的流域上，如果發生交戰的狀況，必須進行軍事調查以確保軍方確實遵守交戰協議，違規者則要面對軍事法庭。但事實上這些都只是表面功夫，並沒有實際上的效用。在《Swift Boat at War in Vietnam》一書就鮮明地紀錄這些事蹟。

當時一艘美軍的快艇曾對著經過的岸邊渡口開槍，附近還有一般平民，這未經許可的行動引起施亞努王子嚴厲的抗議，他當時是獨立柬埔寨的領導人。被指控的美軍宣稱他的行動是正當的，因為他那時正遭受左岸的人開槍攻擊。如果是近距離與敵軍開戰交火，是可以暫時忽視邊界，直到停火為止。簡單來說這條河在五十年前曾經發生許多衝突。

我遊這條河的時候一切都很平靜，只是會不時地想到以前曾經閱讀過關於這裡動盪的歷史。那時我才剛進入美國的大學，校園裡充斥著反戰的氣氛。好幾位朋友從越南退伍後，在美國軍人權利法案下進入校園就讀。

一早六點我們就在等候昨天訂好的船來接我們。它應該在面對江城河的河岸飯店前等候我們。河仙市已經從三角洲的一個沿海村莊轉變成為一個小城市了。十七世紀中，滿清打敗了明朝，來自中國廣東的鄭玖為了躲避滿清於是來到河仙市。當時的安南國王（今越南）將這區交給鄭玖管理。直到今天都還可以看到紀念他的寺廟和陵墓。

現在，這城市裡最高的大樓就是我們住的河岸飯店。其他差不多高的大樓幾乎都沒有窗戶，看起來好像倉庫。有些大樓會用陽台跟類似別墅外牆的方式做裝飾。一些會把低樓層當住家，高樓層看起來都像是工廠或倉庫。

然而，這些樓房不是給人使用或是用來儲藏乾貨的，而是為了吸引金絲燕。原本牠們是棲息在沿岸的石灰岩丘陵和島嶼，並在洞穴裡築巢。但現在這些樓房提供了金絲燕棲息的地方。屋頂上的擴音機播放金絲燕的鳴叫聲以吸引牠們進入築巢。擴音機從早到晚不停地播放，就跟川普發推特一樣。

採集燕窩是個古老的傳統，以往在野外採，現在有些則是在室內。燕子唾液築成的燕窩會再被加工和分類。成品的顏色從白色到黃色甚至是紅色都有，據說含有很高的營養價值。頂級的燕窩一公斤可以賣到高達美金一萬元。在河仙市許多富有的人家都是從事這個行業的。

我們的這艘船十分細長，大約有十八呎長。上面有五條長板椅，一條只可以坐一個人。租四小時要美金三十元，這樣的金額只能買到一點點的燕窩。我從閱讀中得知，五十年前巡邏江城河的船是日夜不停歇的。我們的船往上游開了二十分鐘後，岸邊有一個村莊。這村莊裡很多的房子都還是用茅草蓋屋頂和稻草築牆，比較有錢的才會用磚頭或是水泥，只有幾戶用稻草跟磚頭蓋房子。到處都是窄船，看起來應該是他們主要的交通工具。大部分的船都是用玻璃纖維做的，整個早上我只有看到兩艘木製的長船，還有幾艘比較大但是已經破舊了的木造帆船。

Cruising up river / 搭船往上游

村子後面有很多紅樹林和棕櫚樹，但是只有少許的幾顆椰子樹。有很多水鳥，像是白鷺鷥、鸕鷀，還看到了翠鳥。過去這裡應該是一大片森林，但有趣的是，現在只剩下岸邊前幾排的棕櫚樹還保持完整，樹後就是稻田，再後面就是堤防了。把樹砍掉種田對農業社會和經濟上來說都是合理的，但對環境保育卻是不怎樣如意。

有幾次船夫 Khrung 想要帶我們去支流，但是我堅持要在主要的河道上。我才不想要被越戰遺留下來的東西突襲。看著手機上的地圖，我想要追蹤河流最接近或是越過柬埔寨的地方。

一度地圖顯示我們正在邊界上，因此我請 Khrung 停靠河左岸，岸邊有一個生鏽的小棚子。我想要瞭解住在那裏的是柬埔寨人還是越南人。Jing 是位農夫。他和妻子靠著三頭水牛還有幾隻鴨子維生。

Jing next to house / Jing 在房屋旁

Joyous farewell / 歡喜的道別

我指向遠方一間寺廟的頂端問 Jing 我可不可以過去那裏。他搖搖頭說那裏是 Kampuchea，意思是柬埔寨。離岸邊大約五百公尺處有幾間房子。那些房子是屬於柬埔寨的。我們於是討論著應不應該走過去看看，就像我在偏遠的國境常常做的那樣。學會的攝影師李伯達提醒我那裏可能還有地雷。我想了一下，同意他的看法。

走回船上跟 Jing 道別時，突然想起我經常對年輕人的告誡：「你看過那個地方，但是那個地方看過你嗎？」「試著做一些事，不管是多小的都好！」我從包包拿出一包煮熟的栗子，請李伯達遞給 Jing，離開時我們兩個臉上都露出了笑容。船開始往下游走，樹木與村民都漸漸離我遠去，溶入平靜的環境裡。這樣的景象跟五十年前大大不同，那時巡邏快艇一天到晚在上下游穿梭著。

一九七五年四月三十日，就在克里在越南的幾年後，第一輛坦克車開進了西貢（現在的胡志明市）。美國特工直升機從屋頂撤退了最後的一群越南和美國人。當時紅色高棉軍隊正準備大膽前進佔領河仙市外的小島－富國島。那是越南最大的離島，當時應該屬於南越政權。

歷史上富國島曾屬於越南也有時屬於柬埔寨，須看當時誰的國力比較強。雖然二十世紀大多是屬於越南，但是柬埔寨還是企圖佔領。紅色高棉在一九七五年五月一日占領這個島，但是很快的越軍又將它奪回。兩個共產政權之間的爭奪不斷，直到一九七九年，越南侵入柬埔寨，佔領了快要十年後才撤退，之後兩國關係才逐漸緩和，情勢趨於穩定。

有個很特別的理由吸引我們去富國島參觀。我聽說世界上最好的魚露產自這裡，純度 45 度並且很有年份的魚露。首先將鯷魚浸泡在滷水裡，然後再放入二米到四米高用木頭和藤做的桶子內發酵。這魚露有些人很喜歡，有些人很排斥。曾經有一位越南作者寫過，老漁夫們會在出遠洋前先喝一杯

魚露來保暖，潛水員也會先喝一杯再跳進冰冷的海水裡。這年份甚至可以跟法國葡萄酒和義大利橄欖油相提並論。

我們在早上六點先搭上渡輪，然後在一個半鐘頭的水翼船後，抵達了富國島東岸的碼頭。我們租了一台計程車前往島的最南端，七小時只要美金三十元。在安泰市靠近漁港的地方有一家叫做 *Phung Hung* 的公司專門生產魚露。到了停車場我一下車就聞到濃濃的魚露味。接下來一個鐘頭我不管走到這公司的哪個地方，不管是在工廠裡還是商店，空氣裡滿滿的都是這個氣味。

一大桶一大桶的鯷魚放在廠房發酵，非常壯觀。做桶子的木頭很特別，是本地產的，但是越來越稀少，所以已經禁止砍筏了。據說這種紅褐色的桶子可以讓魚露發酵的更好。鯷魚與滷水的比例是三比一，需要發酵一到兩年。除了鯷魚，也可以用沙丁魚跟鯖魚來做魚露，只是成本會高很多。

我在禮品店碰到了這家族事業的經理 *Kim*。她跟我介紹好幾款他們的魚露。魚露規格從 *30* 度到 *40* 度不等，最高的甚至到 *45* 度。

Barrels of fish sauce / 一桶桶的魚露
Sample tasting / 試喝
Bird's nest at shop / 店裡的燕窩

這些度數代表氮的含量，含量越高越純，味道也更濃郁。通常第一道蒸餾產出 45 度魚露，之後再加入滷水，產出的度數就會降低。他們請我嚐看看純度最高的魚露，用一根小吸管沾一下小碟子。第一口就嗆到我了，讓我喉嚨縮緊。瞬間，我這七十歲的味蕾好像都被喚醒了過來。

我後來買了兩箱 *Phung Hung* 魚露。小瓶的像小酒瓶那樣，可以送給那些勇於嚐鮮的朋友。而我必須承認已經喜歡上這特殊的味道，甚至有點上癮了。禮品店將我買的魚露包了兩層，據說如果在飛機上打破了，會被視為刑事犯罪，就像帶榴槤上飛機一樣。

接下來我去安泰尾端的漁港，剛好碰上漁船正在岸邊卸下漁獲。雖然富國島的觀光業發展的很快，海灘飯店和渡假村一一林立，但很明顯的，漁業才是富國港重要的經濟活動。這裡的機場最近才變成國際機場，可以從曼谷飛進來。

回到碼頭後趕上了最後一班渡輪，下午三點半從富國港出發到河仙市。我可以停留的時間很短暫，不想重蹈中國國民黨的經驗！一九四九年當國民黨的蔣介石撤退到台灣時，約有三萬多軍人從中國被迫退到越南，最後到了富國港，這些人被困在島上三年，最後在一九五三年被法國遣送回台灣。我在這裡只有不到一天的時間，但是已經有很棒的體驗了，包括嘗試世界上最棒的魚露。

登上渡輪時，我的口袋裡有一小瓶 *Phung Hung* 魚露。如果暈船的話，我就喝一口來讓自己舒服點，又或者，就直接讓我昏過去吧！

伊洛瓦底江上的冒險

ESCAPADE
ON THE IRRAWADDY

CERS Riverside House, Mandalay –
October 27, 2019

ESCAPADE ON THE IRRAWADDY
So I thought!

My first and second trips to Prague were exactly ten years apart, in 2009 and 2019. On both trips, I admired a simple drawing by Jiri Votruba, showing a pair of crossed legs in the foreground, a cup of coffee next to the legs, with the Charles bridge and townscape of Prague in the distance. For years, I have taken pictures, like what are today called "selfies," of my own feet in front of nice scenery that I enjoyed. Of course, I take similar images of the scenery, but without my feet. Those pictures are more civilized and fitting for publication to illustrate my writings.

Recently, I met a young artistic friend. We exchanged through WhatsApp her surrealistic paintings and my scenic photos, usually with my feet crossed in front of the beautiful image, be it a sunrise or pristine landscape. Surely my pictures are anticlimactic. Nonetheless the intention was to include myself in the scene; not my face, as everyone loves to do with selfies, but my feet.

Today, big data and big brother are constantly stealthily watching from behind supercomputers that analyse everything we do, probing into the tiniest details of our private lives. It is to be expected that if you watch or download porn, you soon receive porn ads on your phone or computer. If you

Painting by Votruba / Votruba 的畫作   Scenic Irrawaddy / 美麗的伊洛瓦底江

Google a particular type of ailment to learn more, soon big pharma will follow with more tips and sales help. I checked online a potential vacation, and hotels in that region automatically popped up later on. I remember searching for more information regarding the Oshkosh Airshow, which I had visited three times in the past. For the next two months, I received advertising for flight schools and other flight related information.

But here is something new, and very interesting; the analysis of my physical condition through pictures, that of my feet, which I had been circulating just to one recipient. Suddenly, I began to receive via my email much unsolicited advice for sufferers of toe fungus. Ignacio wrote me on "Best at home nail fungus removal" and Christina suggested "Obtain perfect looking toes in as little as 15mins." Roland and Donald competed in proposing "How to remove nail fungus in 48 hours." If I type "fungus" in my email inbox search-bar, I can retrieve 26 toe or nail fungus emails received within the last month, from September 26 to October 26.

Isn't that something, the forensic study of my photos! Soon, the reflection in my eyes will reveal who was the companion taking a picture of me. I always thought my personal pet in the form of my "Hong Kong Foot" was somewhat private. But somehow it has now become public domain! Facial recognition? That's cliché and passé. Footsie recognition is now the new deal. Now I am thinking hard and creatively what to include in my next round of photos for circulation. In short, internet that was once peaceful has changed manipulative, and even aggressive and divisive like in the recent case in Hong Kong. Today, internet is like a toxic drug. You can become addictive and face your own risk. After all, didn't we all sign up to use it with those tiny print of conditions, compromising our privacy. Even the Yes or No boxes are put closely together, waiting for your fingers to inadvertently make the wrong touch.

Convenience of technology always comes with a price, at times not through charges, but by giving away our privacy. But let's go to happier and perhaps more private ground, the upper Irrawaddy on our own CERS boat. Though getting online even from this remote a place would reveal my whereabouts, not to mention that I have been using a global positioning app called Galileo, entering our anchoring position, supposedly just for my own record. And obviously, I'll be entering my cabin tonight with an uninvited companion hidden inside my mobile phone.

Sunset Irrawaddy / 伊洛瓦底江的日落

Flood line / 淹水線
Dam gate machinery / 水壩閘閥的機器設備
Boats on Mu River / 穆河上的船

It took us one full day sailing from Mandalay upriver for about 200 kilometers to get to Male, a small town since British colonial days. I had hoped to rent a four-wheel-drive and head east inland to the mining town of Mogok. There is gold mining, copper mining, or marble quarrying in many parts of Myanmar, but Mogok stood out among all mining in the country by its supremacy in ruby and sapphire mining. Ruby and jade are two rare gems for which the country is famous, and their excavation dates back centuries if not millennia. Sadly, a visit would have to wait for another trip. We did ask, but no one would risk taking us to the mines without a government permit, which could only be gotten from Yangon, Mandalay, or the capital in Naypyidaw. So, I decided to go west instead, exploring another river system, the Mu River near the town of Muwa.

As we moored near Male the previous evening, it was natural that we visited the morning market at Male early on. Though it was small, hosting only two to three teahouses, the street venders in shops, stalls or on the ground were very colorful. As a rule, and with no exception here, I chose a local teahouse to savor my Myanmar milk tea for the morning among the locals. Of course, I had my longyi on in order to blend in. One thing perhaps worthy to point out to serious photographers of markets - I always carry only my small camera. A professional size one would be too intrusive and intimidating, rarely providing a good opportunity to take candid *photos. A well-captured low-res photo is worth far more than one that is high-res, multi-MB, but lousy!*

After the market, it took us two hours by car to reach the Mu River. We stopped first at a dam built by the British in 1902, and completed in 1905. When we got on top of the rather low barrage, perhaps some ten meters above the rapid flow of the river below, I inspected some of the mechanical machinery that raised and lowered the flood gates. The inscriptions revealed that they were manufactured in 1928 in England. Locals said the dam was repaired by the Japanese during World War II, when this area fell under Japanese occupation.

Unlike the much larger dam that had now been constructed on the upper Mu River for the twin purpose of hydroelectric power and irrigation, the dam here was built strictly for irrigation of nearby farmland. Canals and channels radiating out from this dam had benefited the region's many agriculture fields for over a century.

We rented two wooden row boats to go a short distance up the Mu River, above the dam. Our village oarsmen told us that we were the very first outside visitors to come, and no one had ever rented their boats before. Along the way, we saw many wonderful waterfowl, including herons, egrets, cormorants, wild ducks and even a pair of Pied Kingfisher. We stopped to chat with Saw Myo Awing while he was pulling in his net. He got a foot-long Tilapia fish this time around, but told us two years ago he once netted a large fish weighing 30 viss (just short of 50kg) and measuring about two meters, as indicated by spreading his two arms to illustrate the length of his catch.

Next we visited Paze, a pottery village some half hour away on a road infested with pot-holes. Our car scratched its bottom uncountable times, heading there and back. The pottery were basic utilitarian jars to serve as water containers or for cooking, with a minimal cost of 300 Kyat, approximately US20 cents. Multiple pieces were

Myoma Mosque / Myoma 清真寺

discounted at five for 1300 Kyats or under US$1. We bought one pot with a cover, as the bumpy ride was worthy of a souvenir.

Back at Zigon, the small town east of Muwa where the dam was located, train tracks ran through the middle of town. We were lucky on our way in and out, arriving just as the gate came down at the railroad crossing. I was able to observe a freight train hauling over a dozen freight cars of newly felled giant logs from the north. On the way out, a passenger train went by and in front of my eyes passed freight cars full of people standing or squatting, labelled Ordinary Class, followed by only one single carriage for seated passengers.

There was a spectacular mosque in town. Given it was a Friday, I made a stop just in time to see the Muslim observers filing out of the mosque at 1pm after the service. As I was in my shorts and sandals, I could not enter the main building but sat outside for tea with two of the young Islamic teachers while a small crowd looked on.

Sayar Paw Oo and Bo Bo Tun were both young chaps and very friendly, though in the beginning they were somewhat apprehensive as to why someone from as far away as Hong Kong would be interested in their mosque. The ice thawed after I used Google to show them that I had authored a book on Islam in China. That had always seemed to work better than my passport visa, time and again, whenever I needed to talk to someone in a Muslim community.

The Myoma Mosque, looking very new, with glossy tiles walls and several spiral towers to complement the minarets, was constructed and finished in 2000. There were over 170 Islamic families in this town with a population of over 900 Muslims. On any Friday, over 300 men would attend services at their mosque. In all, there were over 15 people who had made the pilgrimage to Mecca. Just last year three more people here gained the honorific title of Haj, having each spent seven million kyat on the trip (US$4,500 plus).

After nightfall, we made it back in time to get on our boat and get ready to start sailing downriver homeward the next day. It would take us half the time going with the flow of the river, or slightly over half a day, to get back to Mandalay, sailing back to our new Riverside House (or Riverside Club if we want to sound important and exclusive). From here, we could reach home in Hong Kong by mid- afternoon the following day.

From Male, we started sailing very early in the morning. I remember looking at the predawn sky changing colors. I told myself then that when I reached Mandalay, perhaps I should spend a little time looking for a spa to have a pedicure and have my toe nails painted in rainbow colors like the morning sky. If I send a picture to a friend, maybe when I next check online, they will be peddling nail polish, or some lovely sandals to match my somewhat improved and beautified feet. But when I checked my mobile phone after leaving it next to my bed for the night, I suddenly saw I have received several new emails, from Jo Cooper and Helen Gonzalez, both offering remedy for my snoring. One Roberto Quinn even offered to save my marriage, through his anti-snoring product. Smart phone certainly come with surprises, I must admit.

伊洛瓦底江上的冒險 我以為是！

我第一次跟第二次去布拉格剛好相隔十年，分別在二零零九年跟二零一九年。兩次我都很欣賞 *Jiri Votruba* 的畫作，在其中一幅畫裡，前景是一雙交叉的雙腳，旁邊放著一杯咖啡，遠處則是查理橋和布拉格的風景。多年來我會在我喜歡的景色前拍我的雙腳，也算是今天大家所說的「自拍」。當然我也會拍沒有我雙腳的風景照。這些照片優雅些，也比較適合放在書裡來為我的文字做說明。

最近我認識一位年輕的藝術家。透過 *WhatsApp* 她發給我她畫的超現實主義繪畫，我則寄給她日出或是美麗的風景照，通常我會交叉雙腿當作前景。當然我拍照的風格不是主流的，不過這目的只是把我自己放進去，而不是把我的臉放進去，像大家自拍那樣，我的自拍一定是拍我的腳。

今天大數據和老大哥偷偷地躲在高速運算的超級電腦後，分析我們做的每件事，探究我們私人生活中的支微末節。如果你在電腦上看過或下載過色情影片，很快你就會在手機或是電腦收到情色廣告。如果你 *Google* 過某種疾病，馬上就會有藥廠送給你相關知識和商品資訊。我曾經在網路上找過一個度假地方，之後那裏相關的飯店資訊隨即跳出來。我也曾搜尋過奧什科甚航空展，我去參觀過三次。接下來兩個月我不斷收到飛行學校廣告還有相關的資訊。

有件新鮮事非常有趣，就是透過照片來分析我的身體狀況，我曾寄給一位朋友我的腳丫子照片。突然間我的 email 收到不知道是誰寄的信，給我關於腳趾真菌的建議。依那丘寫給我「去除灰指甲最好的方法」，克里斯汀娜建議「只要十五分鐘就可以擁有好看的腳趾頭」。羅林和當諾爭相提議「如何在四十八小時內去除灰指甲」。在我的收信箱搜尋「真菌」，光是從九月二十六到十月二十六一個月的時間就有二十六封關於灰指甲或是腳趾真菌的郵件。

是不是很了不起！如同法醫一般地分析我的照片。很快地，我眼睛裡的倒影就將透露出是誰拍我的了。我一直認為我的「香港腳」是很私密的。但是不知道為什麼居然變成公共財！人臉辨識？那已經太過時了。人腳辯識才是新玩意。我認真的在想，充滿創意的去想，下次究竟要放什麼樣的照片好讓它流傳出去。網際網路曾經很平靜，但是已經變得算計，有侵略性，也分歧，就像最近香港發生的事。今天網路像是毒藥。上癮的要自負後果。畢竟我們不是都簽證同意了那一大串密密麻麻法律條文嗎？我們早就對我們的隱私做了妥協。同意跟不同意的按鍵靠得那麼近，目的不就是等著手指頭一不小心就按錯嗎？

HM Explorer / HM 探險號　　　　　　　　　　　　　　　　Breakfast on boat / 船上吃早餐

Preparing tea / 泡茶
Market noodle shop / 市場裡的麵攤
Market food stand / 市場裡的小吃攤

科技帶來的便利是要付出代價的，付出的不是金錢，而是我們的隱私。讓我們去一個開心一點，隱私多一點的地方吧。伊洛瓦底江的上游！搭乘探險學會的船過去。即使是在這麼偏遠的地區上網，即便只是為了記錄而輸入我們的定點位置，都會透露我的行蹤。更不用說我用的是全球定位應用程式伽利略了。看來今晚回我的船艙時，還會有一個不請自來的同伴躲在我的手機裡呢。

從曼德勒往上游航行了一整天，大約兩百公里才到 Male，一個英國殖民過的小鎮。我原本想要租一台四輪驅動車前往東邊內陸的 Mogok 採礦城，但很可惜，因為沒有政府給的許可，所以沒有人敢帶我們去。而許可證要到仰光、曼德勒或是首都內比都才能申請。緬甸有金礦、銅礦還有好多個大理石採石場，而 Mogok 在採礦業中脫穎而出，挖採的是紅寶石和藍寶石。緬甸的紅寶石和藍寶石可是出了名的稀有寶石，採這些寶石的歷史可以追溯到幾世紀前，甚至可能是千年前。因此我決定只好往西走，去探索另一條河系，Muwa 鎮附近的穆河。

前一天傍晚我們在 Male 附近停靠，沒有例外，當然要去他們的早市看看。市場雖然很小，只有兩三家茶館，但是街頭的小販，商店、攤販都很有趣。一如往常，我選了一家當地的茶館跟當地人一起品嚐緬甸奶茶。為了融入，我身上穿的是緬甸人所穿的筒裙。關於攝影，值得一提的是我總是會隨身帶著一台小相機。專業用的相機尺寸太嚇人了，很難捕捉到自然的照片。低解析度的好照片，遠勝過高解析度但是拍不好的照片。

逛完了市場，我們花了兩個鐘頭的車程到穆河。先去看了英國人建造的水壩，這個工程在一九零二年開始，一九零五年完工。我們爬上攔河壩，離下面湍急的河水約十公尺，我查看操控防洪閘門開關的機械。上面寫著一九二八年，英國製。當地人說二戰的時候日本人曾經維修過，因為日本人佔領過這個地方。

跟穆河上游剛蓋好用來發電和灌溉的大水壩不同，這個水壩只為了灌溉附近的農田。灌溉渠道從這裡將水運送到這區域的農田已經超過百年了。

我們租了兩艘木製的划艇到穆河上游不遠處，就在水壩的上方。划船的村民說我們是第一批來這裡的外人，從來沒有人跟他們租過船。一路上我們看到好幾個很漂亮的水鳥，有蒼鷺、白鷺鷥、鸕鶿、野鴨，甚至還有一對斑魚狗。*Saw Myo Awing* 在收網的時候我們停下來跟他聊天。這天他抓到一條一呎長的吳郭魚，兩年前

Male tea house / Male 的茶館
Male fruit stand / Male 的水果攤

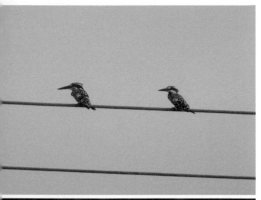

Pair of Kingfisher / 一對翠鳥
Egret in flight / 空中飛翔的白鷺鷥
Saw Myo Awing with his fish / Saw Myo Awing 和魚

他曾抓過一尾重達三十 *Viss*（快五十公斤），約兩米長的魚，他邊說邊把雙手張開來形容那條魚的大小。

接下來我們去了 *Paze*，一個製陶的村莊，開車大概花了半個鐘頭。路上到處坑坑洞洞的，去程跟回程，車子的底盤不知道被刮了多少次。這裡做的陶器多是實用的容器，像是用來裝水的或是用來煮飯的，很便宜，一件只要三百緬幣，約美金二十分。一次買五件還有折扣，折扣後只要一千三緬幣，還不到一美金。我們一路顛簸好不容易來到這，所以買了一個鍋子外加蓋子當做紀念品。

回到 *Zigon*，位於 *Muwa* 東邊的小鎮，也是水壩所在的位置。在這裡火車軌道從市鎮中央穿過。我們去跟回程都很幸運，抵達的時候剛好看到拖著十幾節車廂的貨運火車，載著剛從北部砍伐下來的巨木。回程時一輛載客的火車又剛好經過，載貨的車廂塞了滿滿的人，有人站著有人蹲著；只有標示「普通」的一節載客車廂，乘客才有座位可以坐。

城裡有一座很壯觀的清真寺。這天是禮拜五，剛好一點的禱告結

Log train / 運送木材的火車

Minaret towers / 宣禮塔
Bobo on left next to Sayar / 左為 Bobo，旁邊是 Sayar
Pottery village / 製陶的村莊

束，穆斯林信徒們正排隊從清真寺走出來。因為我穿短褲跟拖鞋所以沒有辦法進去主建築物，只好在外面跟兩位年輕的穆斯林老師喝茶，旁邊還有一小群人圍繞著我們。

雖然 *Sayar Paw Oo* 和 *Bo Bo Tun* 兩位年輕人都很友善，但是一開始的時候還是難免有點緊張，他們不知道為什麼這位遠從香港來的人會對他們的清真寺有興趣。我 *Google* 了我寫的那本關於在中國的伊斯蘭一書讓他們知道之後，氣氛才變得輕鬆起來。每當我到穆斯林社區要找人聊天時，這招是非常管用的，比護照簽證管用多了。

二千年建造並完工的 *Myoma* 清真寺看起來非常新，光滑的磁磚牆和迴旋塔襯托著宣禮塔。這裡約有超過一百七十個穆斯林家庭，人數大約九百多人。每個禮拜五都會有超過三百位男士來清真寺禮拜。總共有十五人曾經到過麥加朝聖。去年有三位得到哈吉的榮譽稱號，每個人需要花費七百萬緬幣去朝聖（至少要美金四千五百）。

入夜後我們及時趕上船，準備隔天往下游回家去。順著河流航行只要花一半的時間，大概只要半天的時間就能回到曼德勒，回到我們新的河畔屋。或是「河畔俱樂部」，如果想要聽起來比較尊貴的話。從那裡出發，隔天下午就可以回到香港。

我們一大清早就從 Male 開船出發。我記得日出前天空色彩的變化。我告訴自己到曼德勒的時候或許應該找一家美容水療館來做一下腳指甲，把它們塗成彩虹般，就像清早的天空那樣。如果我把那樣的照片寄給朋友，當我再上網時應該會看到賣指甲油的，或者是可愛的拖鞋來搭配我美麗的雙腳。我把手機放在床邊，過了一夜，結果當我再拿起它來看時，有好幾封從 Jo Cooper、Helen Gonzalez 還有 Guadalupe Wong 寄來的郵件，竟然都是幫忙我解決睡眠打呼的方法。我必須承認，智慧型手機真的挺能讓人驚喜的。

Ordinary Class train / 普通車廂

回顧探險第一個十年

First Decade of
Exploration Highlights

Mandalay, Myanmar - Sept 5, 2019

First Decade of Exploration Highlights

I have just turned 70, and my exploration has reached five decades. It seems proper to say I began my real exploration in 1969, when I left home for America and college.

Curiosity notwithstanding, throughout my upbringing for the first two decades of my life, I could only explore around my immediate vicinity of Hong Kong. It was when I left home that I could physically explore beyond the place of my childhood. And that, I did.

Looking back on fifty years, I reminisce some of the highlights, both in years, months and days. The rainbow of colors and memories are too rich to recount in detail. Through pictures however, I felt such recall could be captured to a degree of time past, and be shared with a few friends.

That culmination of pictures became this first of a series of five books "Life as an Explorer", a very limited edition of only 500 copies, with merely 200 available for the market. Each book would cover a decade of my exploration work. The book has 425 images, and at a few intervals included Chinese poems I wrote in the 1970s and early 1980s.

The early years of work, including those for the National Geographic, are rarely seen. They are included within pages of the book. Here I have chosen a dozen or so images for sharing. Film in those days was a rare commodity, in limited supply.

Selfie was unheard of in those days. Pictures of myself was almost nil. I recalled on my first trip to China in 1974. In 28 days of travel, I did not have one picture taken of myself. In my first ten years of exploration, I probably have only a dozen or so pictures taken of myself. It seems proper to include some of them here, to reflect on my younger days while in the field.

Dilapidated Great Wall in 1974 / 一九七四年凋零的長城

Hong Kong street food in the 1970s /
一九七零年代香港街邊的小吃攤
Fishing junk of Hong Kong in the 1970s /
一九七零年代香港的漁帆船

Mother with three babies in Guizhou / 母親和三個小孩，貴州
Production at pottery factory / 製陶工廠的生產線

Day care school / 幼兒園
Gymnast practicing school, Shanghai / 上海的體操學校

Machu Pichu in 1975 / 一九七五年的馬丘比丘
Llama at Machu Pichu / 馬丘比丘的駱馬

Living Old Town (Lijiang) in 1981 / 舊城（麗江）於一九八一年
Sumtsaling Monastery at Zhongdian in 1981 /
一九八一年中甸的松贊林寺

A Yi nationality at Liang Shan of southern Sichuan /
四川省南部涼山的彝族姑娘
Tibetan school kids on northern Sichuan /
在四川北部的藏族學童

Tibetan school kids on yaks / 氂牛上的藏族學童

Dragon boat race in Guizhou, 1983 / 一九八三年在貴州的龍舟比賽
Oroqen family in Inner Mongolia, 1983 / 一九八三年內蒙古的鄂倫春族

Monks at Labrang monastery, 1982 / 一九八二年拉卜楞寺的僧人

HM and friend Edward in Central America /
HM 和友人 Edward 在中南美洲
At Tikal, Guatemala / 瓜地馬拉的蒂卡爾

Photographing Llama at Machu Pichu /
在馬丘比丘拍攝駱馬
Backpacking across border / 背包旅行跨過邊境

Camping in Guangxi/Guizhou border / 在廣西貴州邊境露營
On camel in 1979 / 一九七九年在駱駝背上

On train to Mongolia / 往蒙古的火車上
Riding on reindeer of the Ewenki / 騎鄂溫克族的馴鹿

Border crossing with backpack from Peru into Ecuador /
背包旅行從祕魯到厄瓜多

Magazine vender at Cuzco Peru / 祕魯庫斯科的雜誌小販

Crescent Moon Spring in Dunhuang / 敦煌的月牙泉

回顧探險第一個十年

我剛年滿七十歲，探險生涯來到第五個十年。應該說，從我一九六九年離家到美國讀大學的時候，我的探險生涯就開始了。儘管再怎麼好奇，二十歲之前我也只能在香港附近探險。離家後我可以探險的範圍擴大了，遠超越年少時的地方。所以，我便繼續探險。

回看這五十年，讓我想起一些故事，一些年月日。雖然無法一一細數那記憶和豐富的色彩，但是我覺得透過照片多少可以和一些朋友分享那個年代的樣貌。

這些照片集結起來成為《Life as an Explorer》五本系列攝影集中的第一本，限量發行五百本，但在市場上流通的還不到兩百本。每本攝影集都將涵蓋我每十年的探險工作。第一本有四百二十五張照片，從七零到八零年代初期，中間還穿插一些我寫的中文詩。

有一些早期的照片是為美國《國家地理雜誌》拍的，非常罕見。而這些也收藏在攝影集裡。我選了十幾張和大家分享。底片在那年代可是珍貴稀有的資源。那年代根本沒有聽過自拍，所以沒有一張我自己的照片。我記得一九七四年第一次去中國，二十八天裡沒有出現任何一張我的自拍照或被拍照。探險的第一個十年大概只有十來張照片裡面有我，因此挺適合放幾張在裡面，看看我年輕時在野外的模樣。

依
揚
想
亮 出版書目

國家圖書館出版品預行編目 (CIP) 資料

齊物逍遙 2019 / 黃效文著.
-- 初版 . -- 新北市：依揚想亮人文 , 2019.12
　面；　　公分
ISBN 978-986-97108-4-8（精裝）
1. 遊記　2. 世界地理

719　　　　　　　　　　　　　　　　　108021777

齊
物
逍
遙 2019

作者‧黃效文｜攝影‧黃效文｜發行人‧劉鋆｜美術編輯‧Rene｜責任編輯‧王思晴｜翻譯‧依揚想亮
人文事業有限公司｜法律顧問‧達文西個資暨高科技法律事務所｜出版社‧依揚想亮人文事業有限公
司｜經銷商‧聯合發行股份有限公司｜地址‧新北市新店區寶橋路 235 巷 6 弄 6 號 2 樓｜電話‧02 2917
8022｜印刷‧禹利電子分色有限公司｜初版一刷‧2019 年 12 月（精裝）｜ ISBN‧978-986-97108-4-8｜
定價 1200 元｜版權所有　翻印必究｜ Print in Taiwan